TRANSFORMING WHILE PERFORMING

How organisations can find their North Star and get everyone to act in days, not months

Kristof Braekeleire & Olivier Van Duüren

BISPUBLISHERS

T0299478

BIS Publishers
Borneostraat 80-A
1094 CP Amsterdam
The Netherlands
T +31 (0)20 515 02 30
bis@bispublishers.com
www.bispublishers.com

Copyright © 2023 Kristof Braekeleire and Olivier Van Duüren.

Published by BIS Publishers.

All rights reserved. No part of this publication may be reproduced or transmitted in any form
or by any means, electronic or mechanical, including photocopy, recording or any information
storage and retrieval system, without permission in writing from the copyright owners.

Every reasonable attempt has been made to identify owners of copyright. Any errors or
omissions brought to the publisher's attention will be corrected in subsequent editions.

Cover design, book design & layout: Thomas Van Ryckeghem.
Cover illustration, illustrations, templates & comics: Kristof Braekeleire.

ISBN 978 90 636 9672 6

www.visualsenseformers.com
www.thedualarity.com
www.jixso.com

For Heidi, Manon, Dries,
Thomas, Talitha and Lou.

Olivier

For Keira, Megan
and Jessica.

Kristof

ENDORSEMENTS

An inspiring and practicable guide to help you kickstart lasting transformation - and have fun along the way.

Stephen Quest, Director-General Joint Research Centre (JRC) at the European Commission

A leader's compass for the transformation journey. Packed with structured frameworks and fueled with experience and ideas, this book supports learning, coaching and teamwork on the journey. Great resources for moving forward - now where do you want to go?

Madeline Martyn, Learning Consultant

In today's rapidly evolving world, mastering the art of transforming while performing is essential for success. This book expertly guides you through the process, breaking down the necessary skills into simple, practical steps. Whether you're already navigating the challenges of transformation or just getting started, this book is a lifesaver, providing invaluable insights and support every step of the way for organisations to succeed.

Andre Christian, Vice President Innovation at SES, a global leading satellite operator

Discover how to transform your organisation into a high-performing powerhouse using visualisation, inspiration, and co-creation.

Dr Max McKeown, Author of The Strategy Book and other influential books

Transforming while Performing is a must-read for anyone who wants to thrive in the fast-changing and competitive world of business. This book offers practical insights, tools, visual inspiration and strategies to help you balance innovation and execution, adapt to changing customer needs, and create a culture of continuous learning and improvement. Whether you are a business leader, a CxO, an entrepreneur or an innovator, you will find valuable lessons and inspiration in this book. Here's a perfect way to find your true North Star.

Stijn Nauwelaerts, Corporate Vice President Human Resources at Microsoft

Transforming while performing is the most challenging balance act. Now more than ever. With this book, Kristof and Olivier demonstrate why you need this balance and how to obtain it. It's great to see all their knowledge brought down to paper in an easy and accessible way.

Wouter Quartier, Head of Digital, Transformation and Platforms at European Broadcasting Union (EBU)

In this volatile, uncertain, complex and ambiguous world we can only succeed with a clear North Star. Olivier and Kristof have perfected the process of defining such a star while having fun along the way. The amazing design and visuals tap into the emotional brain, reducing resistance in the process.

Elke Van Hoof, CEO at Oh My People (a brand of Huis voor Veerkracht). Professor at VUB. Founder at Ally Institute

A big challenge in innovation and change is to align stakeholders and management behind a shared vision and ambitions towards the future. This book helps you do just that. Start by asking the right questions and use the practical tools, insights, and step-by-step guidelines to turn your thoughts into actionable steps towards your North Star. Then, take it a step further and engage people to get the gears in motion.

Esther Gons, venture builder, co-author of The Corporate Startup and The Innovation Accounting book, founder of the GroundControl platform

This book is a roadmap for people who seek to empower their teams and create sustainable success. It sparked and energised our team, to build a future on our solid foundation whilst keeping our human DNA. We want to remain an inspiration for the industry.

Lise Conix, CEO at Torfs, a Belgian shoe retailer recognised as one of Europe's best workplaces

The transforming while performing experience was a breath of fresh air for us. Their visualisation and co-creation techniques inspired us to unlock our full potential as a team, creating innovative technologies for a sustainable world.

Yves Van Rompaey, PhD, Senior Vice President Corporate Research & Development at Umicore, a leading circular materials technology company

As a seasoned visual practitioner, I was immediately drawn to this book, which offers a valuable contribution to the field of visual strategy. The authors' successful use of visuals in real-life situations is noteworthy. This concise and well-organised handbook is not only a great read but also a valuable reference, providing practical tips and advice. I highly recommend this book as a useful resource and encourage readers to apply the practical advice provided.

Martine Vanremoortele, founder of visualharvesting.com

Since engaging The Visual Senseformers in our transformation, they have walked with us on the journey, bringing their unique brand of insights, thought-provoking questioning and incredible visualisation. This book offers insight into their magic in helping an organisation shift its direction of travel, align around a strong purpose and motivate and engage teams.

Steve Collar, CEO at SES, a leading global satellite operator

GenAI is expanding human capacities and will co-produce most of our experiences by 2030. As distinctions between in-person and fully simulated reality blend, we must be more intentional about creating spaces for human interaction. In "Transforming while Performing," the authors take us on an immersive journey to create spaces in the real and in-person that enhance our connectedness, creativity, and collective intelligence. This book is a thorough, well-researched, practiced, and profoundly thought-out field guide for anyone who has struggled to lead with brain and heart.

Maitri O'Brien, author of New Leaders of Change: How Next Generation of Leaders are Transforming Themselves, Their Business and The World with Purpose and Empathy

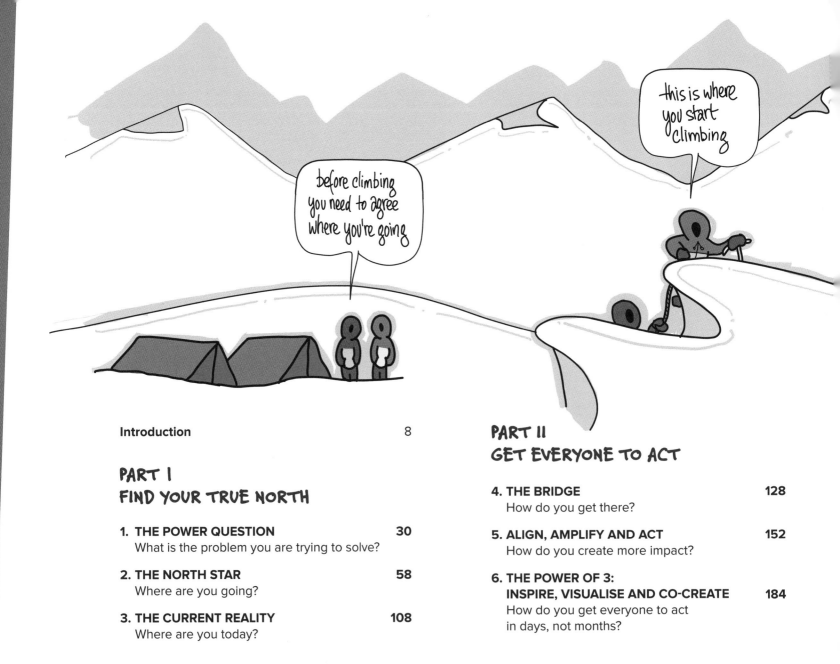

PART III TRANSFORM YOURSELF & YOUR ORGANISATION

INTRODUCTION
Transforming while performing

HOW ORGANISATIONS CAN FIND THEIR NORTH STAR AND GET EVERYONE TO ACT IN DAYS, NOT MONTHS

IT'S LONELY AT THE TOP

When Brie called us she had a huge problem. She had been headhunted for a top job at an intergovernmental organisation serving various member states, quite a step up from her previous position. But she inherited a conflicted team and a culture of distrust. That with the new job put tremendous pressure on her. From her new boss, from her team, and from partners and customers.

Ben saw his AI start-up grow fast but chewed over how he could scale for global impact. He wanted to develop and execute a sustainable vision and strategy with his core team. The key tenets for their transformation towards a scale-up were agreeing on their storyline and their culture to have a positive societal impact with a scalable AI platform.

John became the CEO of his company through an acquisition in the telecommunications industry. He came from an agile culture but now faced a conservative board favouring the status quo despite declining profit margins and massive market shift. He needed to act quickly to manage the uncertainty and get his new global leadership to co-create a new vision for the company.

When asked to think ahead three to five years, Thomas, a senior director of a global tech client, replied: "Three to five years? We think in quarters, maximum one year ahead. Twelve to twenty quarters is really a stretch!"

Sarah had been tasked by the minister of health to create an action plan to address mental well-being at work for her country. This work was commissioned by four ministries and gained high visibility. It had to be validated by experts and needed to engage all main actors in the field. Quite an arduous task, but it also had to be done in less than three months.

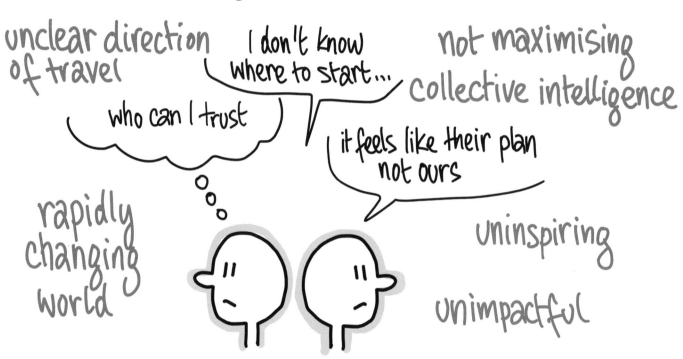

THIS FEELS LIKE THEIR PLAN, NOT OURS!

As visual transformers we run into people like Brie, John, Thomas, Sarah and Ben a lot. Maybe you recognise yourself. Are you stuck? Do you feel lonely at the top and find it hard to trust anyone? Do you sometimes feel like an imposter in spite of your skills and experience? Do you need to come up with a new vision, strategy and culture to be able to succeed? You need to transform but you have no idea how. You find it hard to co-create but you know you can't do it alone. You think you always need to appear like a strong leader.

Meanwhile the world is whirling around you and changing at a pace you've never seen. Changes in the way we work and live. Changes in how we interact with each other as customers, citizens, suppliers, partners, colleagues, family and friends.

These situations are not uncommon. Now more than ever there is pressure on every organisation to **Transform while Performing**. It is extremely challenging to keep an open mind to refresh your future vision and define a direction of travel. As a leader, you want to find out how you can harvest the collective human intelligence to build better strategies and align all stakeholders in a co-creative and inspiring way, so they feel it is their plan, not someone else's. And you need to do it fast? You may even want to turn transformation into a strategic capability? That's exactly what this book is about.

The main question we are trying to answer is "how can organisations find their North Star and get everyone to act in days, not months?" This is the Power Question of the book. More about the use of Power Questions in the first chapter.

HELP ME TRANSFORM WHILE PERFORMING

To stay afloat, companies and governments we've worked with come to us to find a way to transform while performing. They need to run their businesses to bring value today and reinvent their businesses to bring value tomorrow. They want agility and speed and they need everyone on board. They need to execute the present and invent the future. Transforming while Performing is the new normal.

This is no small challenge for incumbents, companies with a legacy, shareholders around the globe, hundreds to thousands of employees and customers, assets worth millions, even billions, proven products and services and established business models. These incumbent companies envy the agility, speed and creativity of smaller entities and start-ups. These smaller players more easily attract skills, culture and entrepreneurship, allowing them to develop new ideas and disrupt entire industries. The larger players may have innovation capabilities, but often lack the ability to transform their operations fast enough into new categories of business.

For those companies transformation is not a strategic capability.

Many incumbents struggle to respond to new entrants in their existing markets. Often their products and services are not what customers want any more. The problem is their existing performing businesses are usually still mostly profitable. They often spot the alarm calls, but fail to respond. It's like they're in a state of inertia. Just like in physics they continue in this state or motion unless that state is changed by an external force. And that is exactly the point.

So ask yourself what is that force that may impact your business in the future? Or is it impacting you already? Does it come from the outside or from the inside?

It could be that you and your teams are blind to the changes around you. That you are not challenging the status quo. You might already be losing key talent or fail to attract new blood. Maybe you are still winning so you don't see the reason to change. It could be you are so focused on the day-to-day that you don't have

transforming   performing

time to truly innovate. You just struggle to make sense of what is happening around you.

Meanwhile on our planet every day 250,000 companies are created, 240,000 are going out of business and 10,000 new patents are being filed[1]. Some of this is happening in your industry, with new players like start-ups that don't play by the rules leveraging new technologies to gain market share. They target your weaknesses as an incumbent. It's possible the entire industry you're in is shifting because of changing consumer trends. You may have been investing in innovation. It might even be that you're on to something ground-breaking but not promoting it yet, because it might damage the sale of your core business. It could be that you are clueless as to how you could interact differently with citizens or customers who are more and more polarised and have a growing public mistrust.

Whatever the reason, if you don't act now, it might be too late. So unless you want to be on the long list of organisations that didn't make it, now is the moment to reassess your vision, your leadership and culture. Now is the time to look into your customer relationships, and the ecosystem you are playing in. And evaluate your talent, your assets, your organisational design, your business models, your market offerings. You need to transform your culture, how you think, operate and interact with your stakeholders while keeping your business running. And you don't have months or years to do it. You need to act now, if not someone else will be eating your lunch. And you need everyone to act and get aligned so they can focus on solving the right problems.

The million-dollar question is how do you find that balance between transforming and performing?

WHY WE WROTE THIS BOOK

We've seen many of our clients struggle with this classic business conundrum: striking the right balance between transforming and performing. Creating new capabilities that transform the business to the next horizon, while running a reliable operational environment for the business. The intensity of one versus the other might vary, and one might be more present than the other during certain periods. It heavily depends on where you are in your journey, where you want to go, what context you are in and what is happening around you. Your current performance fuels your transformation. Your transformation fuels your future performance.

Operational excellence is a mindset that embraces processes and tools to create a culture of excellence within an organisation across the value chain. Innovation excellence similarly is the mindset that embraces processes and tools to create a culture of innovation within an organisation.

Transforming while Performing is not a one-time event, but an ongoing process. Sounds simple. But what's the catch? Focusing only on performance and making operational excellence centre-stage will kill innovation and creativity in your organisation, the essential ingredient for a successful transformation. When performing becomes your purpose, you will cultivate, as time goes by, a talent base of performing experts focused on scorecards, KPI measurement and execution, pushing creative and innovative talent to the basement. In fact, the latter will most probably leave your company and new, creative talent will not want to join your company.

High time you asked yourself: am I able to transform to secure our future and keep performing in the short term?

To be a top performer you need operational excellence.

To be a top transformer you need innovation excellence.

Performing for the short term

Performing mainly revolves around delivering on the commitments you made in the short(er) term. It is your day-to-day performance. It's where you grow the business, operate the supply chain, create cash, deliver on time, create return for shareholders and value for customers, where you develop your company's capabilities, where you improve profit margins, where you acquire a larger market share.

Your focus is on people, customers, profitability, and the society of today. It revolves around enhancing your effectiveness, efficiency and productivity. This is about building credibility, trust and relationships with your customers, partners, co-workers and suppliers. It's where you earn the "right to exist", where you get your "ticket to play".

You obtain all this by striving for operational excellence.

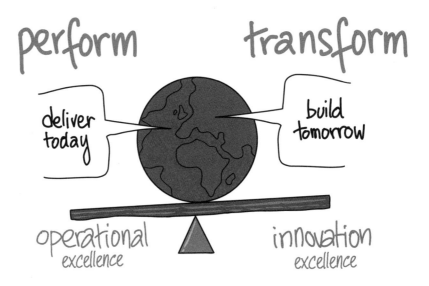

Transforming for the long term

Transforming on the other hand is where you build your future in the long run. It is the power that drives us forward, the belief in our future and is long-term oriented. It is where the true power sits. Analysts, shareholders, customers, employees, contractors want to know whether you have the power and the ability to transform.

People stay longer in a company they believe in. Shareholders evaluate the potential when investing and buy more shares when they believe in the company's future. Customers will buy your products and services when they believe you will be around for a lot longer. Your focus is on people, customers, profit and the society of tomorrow. This is innovation in the broadest sense, not just technology innovation. In Latin, "innovare" means to introduce something new. Something you add to the established rites or customs. Or something that replaces it.

In the context of business performance and transformation, it is about introducing something new to your culture, organisation, technology, products, customer relationships, business models or replacing it by something superior. This is where you reflect on why you transform and how you will get there. This is where you create "breathing" space to incubate new ideas, to innovate, an environment that stimulates ideas, entrepreneurship, and creativity. This is where you create buzz and build communities, where you gain fans for life. This is where you earn your "ticket to win".

You realise this by firming up your innovation excellence.

WHAT YOU WILL LEARN

In this book, you will learn how to get everyone aligned behind your North Star and start acting in days, not months. And you'll discover how you can turn it into a transformation capability for your people and organisation. We'll share real-life cases and stories to inspire you, with visuals that speak more than a thousand words and with practical tools and best practices for you to start co-creating your future together.

The overall structure is the map for your journey. It will guide you through your journey of Transforming while Performing. It's not just business. It's personal!

Overall this book is split into three main parts.

PART I: FIND YOUR TRUE NORTH

The first three chapters describe how you can find your true North and build your vision, strategy and culture and make it better by looking at your current reality.

PART II: GET EVERYONE TO ACT

Chapters 4 to 6, paint a picture of how you can get everyone to act, engaging your wider organisation through inspiration, visualisation and co-creation to fine-tune your North Star and strategy (Bridge) and spread it across the organisation.

PART III: TRANSFORM YOURSELF & YOUR ORGANISATION

The last three chapters, offer you inspiration on the personal, the business and cultural aspects of transformation and on how to turn transforming into performing. Culture transformation is the biggest and the hardest step to get right.

Each chapter fits in the journey map but can also stand on its own. They all address a specific Power Question, focusing on the problem you're trying to solve. The first six chapters are more practically oriented with tools to help you find your North Star and develop an effective strategy and execution. The last three offer you a chance to take a step back and reflect on yourself, your organisation and your culture.

the power question
what question are we answering?

the problem
what is the problem?

the solution
what steps do we need to take?

the reward
what is the impact?

Chapter in brief

Each chapter starts with a short intro on what you will learn and a "chapter in brief" covering the four components: the power question, the problem, the solution and the reward.

In short we'll help you:

- ☑ Find your **North Star**, develop your strategic plan and get everyone to act in days, not months.

- ☑ Sense the world around you and Transform while Performing **as a person and as a business.**

- ☑ **Turn transformation into a strategic capability.**

- ☑ **Unleash the Power of 3**: inspiration, visualisation and co-creation to spark imagination, maximise group genius and accelerate the process.

- ☑ **Get inspired by real-life cases and the visual tools.**

WHO THIS BOOK IS FOR

This book is for anyone that realises the old methods of making plans and strategies for the future are simply not sufficient. To all the leaders, decision makers, entrepreneurs, innovators and change drivers, if you're looking for a better way to build your future and plan your journey together, this book is for you. Get ready to start Transforming while Performing!

This book contains methods and techniques that we adjusted or invented to fit our customers' needs. It includes real-life cases that may trigger you. It contains research to inform you and insights to inspire you. It is powered by stories, research, context, visuals, tools and cases carefully selected to help you find your North Star and get everyone to act in days, not months.

The business cases throughout this book are a selection of some customers we worked with:

Industry: SES, a global leading satellite operator - Torfs, a Belgian shoe retailer - Filou Oostende, a Belgian basketball team - Research & Development Umicore, a leading circular materials technology company

Public Sector: Telecommunications & Integrated Applications, European Space Agency (ESA) - Joint Research Centre, European Commission

Start-up: Swoove Studio, trade name of Intelligent Internet Machines BV (IIM), a 3D animation start-up

We respect the confidentiality of the shared information and ensured that the presented business cases do not compromise sensitive information.

This book is for:

- ☑ Any organisation, new or established, searching for purpose and direction in days, not months.

- ☑ CEOs, leaders, managers, decision makers and entrepreneurs looking for a boost to move away from a traditional way of building and executing their future strategy and vision.

- ☑ HR professionals that are fed up of talking shops and are curious for inspiration on how to do it faster with more impact.

- ☑ Innovators, disruptors, transformers and rulebreakers trying to up their game and seeking fresh inspiration on new ways to transform and innovate rapidly.

- ☑ Start-ups looking to scale to the next level and balance transforming with performing.

- ☑ (Visual) facilitators, students, business schools, consultants and strategic event organisers that are looking for new insights and methods from transformation successes.

WHO WE ARE

When an international business school asked Kristof to visually record Olivier's keynote and workshop for an audience of around a hundred business leaders, something sparked. Both avid fans of Tintin, the well-spirited, open-minded and creative comic book character invented and drawn by Hergé. Both had the same university degree and a similar background in economics, technology, transformation, and entrepreneurial thinking. We're both Belgian and both worked 20+ years for global technology giants and industry pioneers, in different regional entities and in the global headquarters: Kristof at Hewlett-Packard) and Olivier at Microsoft. We have similar values and views on the world and how to make it better. Yet we never crossed paths until we left our corporate life to become independent entrepreneurs, on an adventure of business and personal transformation.

So after that multi-customer workshop for that business school, we sat together to explore what we could do together by merging our strengths and capabilities. In a little under six years, we ran transformation programmes with start-ups, scale-ups, medium to large enterprises in tech, aerospace, raw materials and battery recycling, for public government administrations including finance and treasury, customs, work and pensions, health, and many more. We co-created with over 3,000 participants. It was a rollercoaster. We even planned for this book in 2017, but realised we wanted more joint cases to demonstrate that our approach worked.

Our core activities have taken us all over the planet and include coaching, delivering keynotes, kickstarting transformation programmes, running vision and strategy workshops and visualising the process. We currently advise small and large organisations in all major industries around the world, from start-up to incumbents. Before becoming independent consultants, we were on your side of the table and have the scars on our backs of over forty collective years of experience, good and bad, from organisations that were constantly transforming and facing disruption.

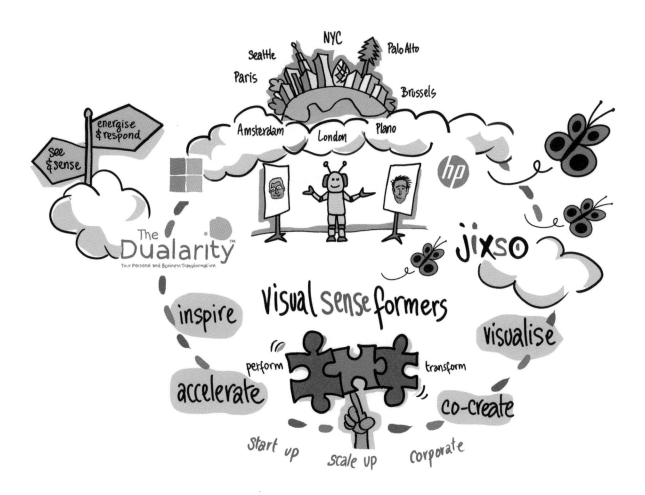

We call ourselves the Visual Senseformers to help organisations and individuals, like you, find their North Star and co-create better strategic plans to get everyone to act in days, not months. We want to help you see and sense today and tomorrow, forming and shaping your senses to start Transforming while Performing. This book combines the power of visualisation, inspiration and co-creation, bundled into a model that you can jump right into, for small, medium and large organisations.

Our focus is not on individuals, but we realised over the years that most of these also apply to personal transformation. We've used them as a guideline for coaching and mentoring individuals.

Our hope is that reading this book will inspire you to find your North Star and start navigating your way through these turbulent times. Just remember, you're not alone.

VISUAL SENSEFORMERS

"Senseforming motivations give participating in an activity personal sense. This kind of motivation is related to values."

We named ourselves the Visual Senseformers because we played around with the words sense, visual and formers, referring to transformer and performer. There was not much science to it. We just liked it. It sounded right.

When we tried to make sense out of it afterwards we found that senseforming motivations give participating in an activity meaning and personal sense. This kind of motivation is related to values. The fact that it had to do with motivation, personal sense and values really appealed to us.

So translated to our world, we became the Visual Senseformers motivating individuals and businesses through inspiration, visualisation and co-creation to accelerate their transformations.[2]

PART I FIND YOUR TRUE NORTH

CHAPTER 1
THE POWER QUESTION
What is the problem you are trying to solve?

What you will learn in this chapter...

Many teams, when confronted with a problem, tend to dive straight into problem-solving. Yet, taking a step back and getting aligned on what problem(s) really need to be addressed and why, simply pays off. In this chapter we'll show you an effective technique using the Power Question to align people so you can focus on solving the right problem(s) which will deliver far more value for your environment.

You don't need to be an expert in analytical troubleshooting or design thinking for this. Using a Power Question can do miracles. This is the first step in defining your North Star.

what is the problem you are trying to solve?
focus
align
Solve the right problem!
the power question
why are we here?
what do we want to achieve?

CHAPTER IN BRIEF

THE POWER QUESTION

What is the problem you're trying to solve?

THE PROBLEM

People tend to dive into problem-solving without having a clear problem statement. As a consequence, too many organisations end up solving the wrong problems.

THE SOLUTION

Align on the big pain points and problem areas before anything. Asking the right questions upfront makes a big difference.

Define the focus of your activities by formulating a simple question, the "Power Question", that articulates what problems you intend to solve.

THE REWARD

A clear list of big problems and the context in which they arise gives the team focus and keeps you on track and provides clarity and focus on the problem(s) that need solving.

1.1 STOP SOLVING THE WRONG PROBLEMS

According to Harvard Business Review, the average executive spends 23 hours a week in meetings, that's more than half your average working week, or in other words half your working life. That number tends to increase the larger the organisation you're working for. Many meetings are so dysfunctional that they represent the single biggest timewaster in the workplace.[3]

"Many meetings are so dysfunctional that they represent the single biggest timewaster in the workplace."

– Harvard Business Review

Part of the problem is we often dive into action without a clear goal or problem statement.

If we had more productive meetings we would save a lot of time to do more meaningful work that has real impact. But dysfunctional meetings are just part of the problem. The real problem is we often act or start new initiatives without a clear goal or problem statement. And rather than investigating the problem, the cause, we dive into problem-solving mode and workshops to fix a problem or a challenge.

So it's no surprise many of us dread these so-called workshops, where sadly too often no real work is done. Or at least no work with impact. We've observed also that few organisations teach their employees how to prepare and run efficient meetings. It's rather crucial though to make sure people understand why they are called to action

and what they are expected to do, before, during and after the meeting. Unproductive task forces and workshops can cause stress, dysfunctional teams and bad employee morale. And this affects not only your planned transformation, but also your performance today.

35

1.2 ENTER THE POWER QUESTION...

These problems could have been avoided if someone asked this very simple question: what is the problem you are trying to solve? Some call it the exam question or focus question. We call it the Power Question. Because asking the Power Question will do miracles. It gives you the power to ask why you need to act and what you are hoping to get out of the action. It gives you the power to get people engaged. It gives you the power to keep people on task, keep them honest.

It's our solution to dysfunctional meetings and ineffective programmes or projects. But, as we said, it goes beyond meetings. Start every transformation with a "Power Question". Use it throughout the life cycle of your programme, your project, your initiative to keep or adjust the focus of your collaboration, your events, your communications. Although it is also useful to structure your own thinking, it is especially powerful for aligning groups during your attempts to co-create, something you'll need to do in every transformation.

Start with a Power Question

A Power Question asks...

- what problem you are trying to solve
- what you are hoping to get out of the action
- whether this is worth spending time on

A Power Question gives you the power to...

- set the scene, context and define the scope
- focus and align on what's important
- bring you back to the task when you've lost track

An effective Power Question links a problem in the present to an outcome in the future. In other words, it asks about the problem you want to address and what you are trying to get out of it. A Power Question can have various iterations as you work your way through the transformation. When your team expands it should be challenged, augmented, commented upon, agreed or disagreed with. That's how you start driving the co-creation during your transformation.

The ingredients of a Power Question

"what or how..." **+** "to..."

The problem	The outcome
The challenge	The opportunity
The action	The value
The journey	The reward
Your focus	Your success

Asking what you need + Asking why you need it

When to use a Power Question?

Phase	When	Why
Planning	whenever you start building a strategy, a project or an action plan	to get clarity on why action is needed
Invitations	when you invite people to contribute	to inform attendees of the focus so they can adequately prepare
Kick-off	when you start any co-creation	to align everyone on the task at hand
Tracking	when the transformation is going off track	to bring everyone back to the initial why
Closing	before wrapping up a project	to evaluate if you've successfully answered the Power Question (as a sanity check)

Let's first look at some real-life Power Questions.
Here's one we created for one of our clients.

This example focuses on:

- what must be done in the present, i.e. resetting your (current) strategy and culture

- to achieve a successful outcome in the future, i.e. to win in the fast-paced world.

In this case the customer left out the problem or their starting point which is fine. Most likely the starting point is an inadequate strategy and culture in a fast-paced world. They did this to keep it simple and to focus on what they want to tackle. Remember the intention is that people who contribute understand the focus and potentially ask additional clarifying questions. Coming up with the right Power Questions is a work of art: don't make them too fluffy, but also not too detailed.

The Power Question should be plain and simple, easy to understand. The answer, in contrast, can be lengthy. As a matter of fact, that's why you need co-creation: to help you answer the Power Question. If you do this right, it will avoid the team diving straight into problem-solving, potentially wasting time and effort if not everyone agrees on the problem to be solved.

TOOL
USING A POWER QUESTION IN CO-CREATION

Step 1: Find the right Power Question

☑ Write down a draft Power Question, trying to answer what problem you are trying to solve and what you hope to get out of it?

☑ Start small, on your own or with two or three co-workers. You may get stuck and need to do some research.

☑ The Power Question should be plain and simple, easy to understand. The answer, in contrast, can be lengthy.

Step 2: Open your co-creation with a Power Question

☑ Start any co-creation with your Power Question. Use the template.

☑ Make people see it: write it on a board or a large sheet of paper.

☑ Make people hear it: before you start, gather around the Power Question, asking them if that is what they want to spend their time on.

Step 3: Capture comments

☑ Capture comments and thoughts on the template.

☑ Take a step back and look at what you've co-created. Read out loud what you've written down.

☑ See if you missed anything.

power question

EXAMPLES CO-CREATION

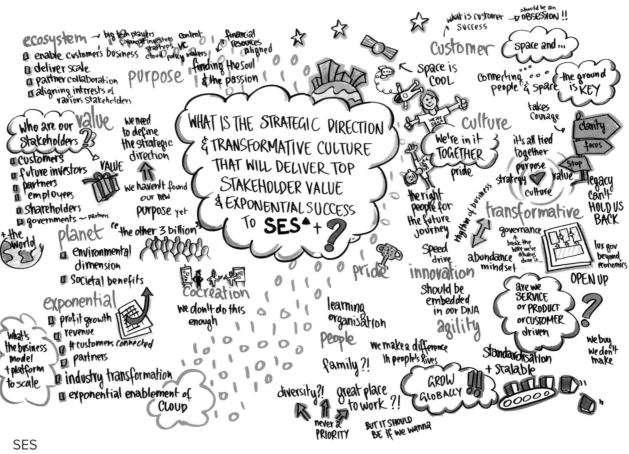

SES
Global leading satellite operator

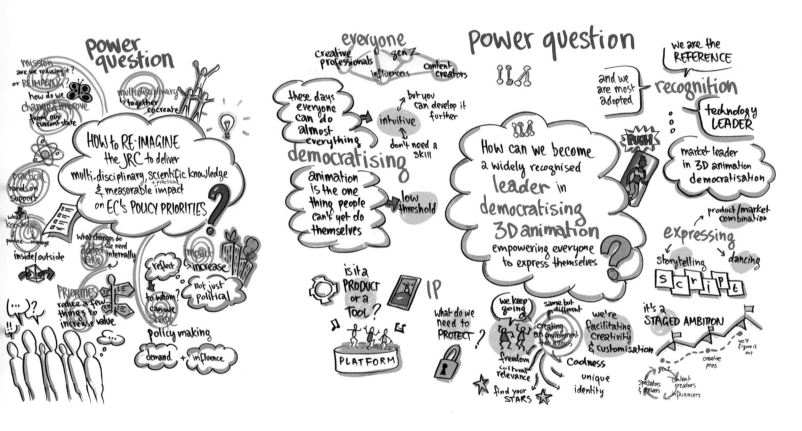

Joint Research Centre (JRC)
European Commission

Swoove Studio, Intelligent Internet Machines
3D animation startup

EXAMPLES CO-CREATION

For inspirational purposes, we've listed seven Power Questions we've co-created with our customers for their transformations. They were focused on resetting their North Star, defining the strategy and aligning everyone. It might help you with yours.

In light blue we've marked what the group wanted to achieve at the end of the workshop and **in white the value it would deliver.**

What is the strategic direction and transformative culture **that will deliver top stakeholder value and exponential success to our company?**

How can our division hit refresh **to help our company remain competitive in a fast-changing world?**

What strategy do we need **to remain the leading player in our industry?**

How to reimagine our organisation **to deliver value that positively impacts policy priorities and outcomes?**

How can we evolve towards a dynamic organisation that uses data **to create societal and economic value?**

What capability and skills do we require **to successfully deliver value to our customers in support of our global strategy?**

How can we build and execute a sustainable vision and strategy **to scale for global AI impact?**

When you open your meeting with the Power
Question, you start with why.

**'If we are starting with the wrong
questions, if we don't understand
the cause, then even the right
answers will always steer us
wrong... eventually.'[4]**

- Simon Sinek

1.3 HANDLING OBJECTIONS

You may come across participants who feel reluctant about the Power Question. Perhaps they don't like to step out of their comfort zone. Or they don't see the need for change. It could be they are afraid and want to protect their jobs, keep things the way they've always done things before. And so they may be trying to avoid the task. Some people are in the programme team for the wrong reasons. They could be obstructing your process. You might argue why they are even part of the team. But they could also be having key information that could lead to critical insights. Or maybe they just need a little more context. The question here is how you handle those that object.

We've listed some objections we've come across. Things people might say because they feel threatened or insecure. And how we suggest you handle them.

"Isn't this the same as listing the objectives?"

A valid question. A Power Question is indeed similar to listing the objectives of a meeting or a programme. But programme objectives are often either too high level or far too detailed. They may even be copied and pasted from another document or made by someone who isn't even involved in the programme.

In contrast, the Power Question sets the scene with the team members and defines the focus for each session, each iteration. It discusses the one thing we want to have achieved after the event. The Power Question therefore shapes the overall programme objectives. People have a natural tendency to jump to action and skip the objectives. Therefore, we find a Power Question is very helpful especially when it includes the problems, referencing the context you are operating in, as well as the desired outcomes, the points you wish to achieve. The table on the next page explains that with practical examples.

49

EXAMPLES CO-CREATION

In blue we've marked what the group wanted to achieve at the end of the workshop and in white the value it would deliver.

GLOBAL TECHNOLOGY COMPANY

Typical meeting objectives

- Review capabilities and skills in support of our EMEA strategy.

- Be open and stretch ourselves.

- Build an effective plan to meet our EMEA objectives.

Power Question

What capability and skills do we require to successfully deliver value to our customers in support of our EMEA strategy?

ICT SERVICES COMPANY

Typical meeting objectives

- Create a winning strategy.

- Secure our position as industry leader.

- Get the group together.

- Challenge our way of thinking.

Power Question

What strategy do we need to remain the leading player in our industry?

NON-GOVERNMENTAL ORGANISATION

Typical meeting objectives

- Create a new strategy with our leadership team.

- Focus on value creation.

- Make choices and define priorities.

Power Question

How do we reimagine our organisation to deliver value that positively impacts policy priorities and outcomes?

GOVERNMENT ADMINISTRATION

Typical meeting objectives

- Become a data-driven organisation.

- Increase agility, but evidence based.

- Create more value for citizens and the economy.

Power Question

How can we evolve towards a dynamic organisation **that uses data to create societal and economic value?**

MANUFACTURING COMPANY

Typical meeting objectives

- Gain buy-in on the vision, strategy and culture of our company.

- Agree how we secure our day-to-day business and future success.

- Create the action plan together.

Power Question

How can we co-create the bridge towards our future to allow us **to Transform while Performing?**

AI SCALE-UP

Typical meeting objectives

- Build a new vision and strategy for our company.

- Enable faster scaling.

- Create AI solutions with more impact.

Power Question

How can we build and execute a sustainable vision and strategy **to scale for global AI impact?**

"No need for a Power Question... we are a senior group."

Maybe you're infallible. We believe we're not. Anyone can make mistakes along the journey, junior or senior. It's how you correct your course that makes you successful. So why waste precious time solving the wrong problems? That's why getting aligned on the why of any meeting or any action is worth it.

Best-case scenario, it takes you a few minutes to agree, and agree quickly and can move on. Worst case, it takes a lot more time and you need a good conversation to fine-tune the problem statement and desired outcomes. Is that so bad? It allows you to tweak the agenda and facilitate the meeting even better. And even if you decide to postpone or cancel an event, is that not better than having a dysfunctional one that does more harm than good.

"That is the way we've always done things around here."

Some groups don't challenge the status quo. They like to stay in what they know, what makes them feel comfortable. It served them well for years and hopefully for many years to come. Looking at the global trends driving change and today's reality, we would beg to differ. So, make sure the Power Question contains an element that points to the outside world. Things like customers, reputation, market perception.

53

"Objectives should be S.M.A.R.T."

Why not make the Power Question S.M.A.R.T., as in specific, measurable, achievable, relevant, and time-bound,[5] you may ask. We find this very valuable, for instance when you document the outcomes of the meeting, but for starting a co-creation exercise, it is too complicated and narrows down the conversation.

The Power Question discussion should be a divergent conversation, not a convergent one. Some argue it could even be emergent, as in imaging the future, the art of the possible. To that purpose we suggest keeping the Power Question simple to define focus and allow people to elaborate what should be part of the discussion and what not.

"How do we know what we don't know?"

Group thinking can be extremely powerful, but also dangerous. That's why it's important to create a safe environment, where you can challenge each other and keep each other honest. It's often more valuable to list what you don't know, and let that inform your action plan, than to base your action plan on a series of non-validated assumptions or statements that were made out of fear of exposing to your co-workers that you didn't have all the answers.

55

What you have learned...

☑ **Align on context and problems:** you've learned how to create a Power Question and how to use it during your meetings to align people on context and problems.

☑ **Increase focus and value:** this will provide line of sight and allow you to get more out of your teams.

☑ **Stay on track:** your Power Question also helps attendees stay on course when teams digress.

Simply put: using a Power Question avoids attendees from solving the wrong problems and aligns them on the task at hand.

When you define your North Star in the following chapter you will need to create your own Power Question before you start your transformation.

CHAPTER 2
THE NORTH STAR

Where are you going?

What you will learn in this chapter...

Transformation is hard. Getting and keeping everyone on board is a challenge. To really know where you're going you need a North Star.

This chapter will help you define your target destination and get everyone going in the right direction. It will guide and inspire you to succeed as an organisation.

CHAPTER IN BRIEF

THE POWER QUESTION

Where are you going?

THE PROBLEM

Do you lack an internal compass or have you lost it along the way? Reimagining or simply resetting your North Star helps you navigate towards what you truly desire and keeps/gets people on board.

THE SOLUTION

To find your North Star you need to answer four key questions:

PURPOSE: Why do you exist?

AMBITIONS: What does your future success look like?

VALUE: What value do you want to create for your stakeholders?

CULTURE: What culture will help you get there?

THE REWARD

A North Star serves as a compass, drives everyone and provides a common direction of travel that informs every action.

WITHOUT A NORTH STAR, PEOPLE TEND TO GET SUCKED INTO THE CHALLENGES AND OPPORTUNITIES OF YESTERDAY AND TODAY CAUSING THEM TO LOSE THEIR SENSE OF DIRECTION.

2.1 WHY YOU NEED TO FIND YOUR TRUE NORTH

You may have recently communicated your strategy, your vision, and all the plans that have been carefully crafted by teams working on various aspects of the transformation to your wider organisation. But you've noticed that employees don't seem to latch on. You wonder why that is.

Did you fail in your communication? Do they really understand why they do what they do? Do they feel it's a top-down decision, pushed by the people who don't understand what's going on? Or is it simply inevitable that most transformations fail?

Many businesses, small and large, struggle to find and align on a future destination and direction of travel that is meaningful and inspiring for everyone. Thinking long term and letting go of the current constraints is tough. People often get sucked into the challenges and opportunities of the day which causes them to lose their sense of direction.

Many don't even have a direction or choose the wrong direction. Others focus on an outdated direction. Some come up with too many directions or continuously keep changing directions.

That's why you need a North Star.

AMBIGUOUS   CLEAR

2.2 YOU NEED A NORTH STAR TO REALLY KNOW WHERE YOU'RE GOING.

The North Star, also called Polaris or Earth's pole star[6], has been used to navigate for centuries, acting as an enchanting light to ensure people are travelling in the right direction. It has served as a reliable beacon to guide seafarers home.

When you build or reimagine your business without establishing a clear North Star first, you and your teams risk losing direction and losing your way. That spreads quickly amongst your staff, as they suffer from not knowing or not finding that beacon of light, which guides them, inspires them, gives them hope.

A North Star can serve **as a compass that drives everyone and every action towards a purpose, a destination.** It's a destination that we can rely on in an ever-changing world. It helps you navigate and prioritise through tough times.

When you find your true North Star, you find your purpose. You know where you're headed, what to do, where to aim, and why it is important. It's like having a picture in front of you of where you want to go. The idea of having a clear sense of direction, intention and an understanding that your contribution is making sense makes you feel energised, inspired and alive. It also makes it easier to make choices and set priorities. It empowers employees to act.

In contrast, not knowing what you and your team stand for, what value you bring, will cause you to stray from your purpose. Not being clear on where you're going or how you work together will hinder you from reaching success. If you don't know what to do and why you do what you do, you will get distracted, and this will cost you time and effort. It will eventually burn you out.

"If your people are clear on a North Star, they are clear on (almost) everything else. It guides them on all of their work, including their micro-actions, micro-routines, and micro-behaviours – without requiring micro-management."[7]

– Gapingvoid

We believe defining your North Star and your future state is a condition to succeed. Doing this helps you build your strategy, your plan, your journey, it enables you to Transform while Performing. Keeping your eyes on the North Star avoids drowning in the day-to-day.

65

It's quite common in business to not take enough time to reflect on one's North Star. Instead, many get stuck in the traditional way of building and adjusting vision and strategies in this rapidly changing world. But how can you do that differently? How do you determine your North Star? How can you even know where you want to be in three to five years or even more? How much time and effort will it take you to find your North Star? And how will you align all your stakeholders? And finally, where do you start?

You might ask yourself how this relates to vision and mission. In business iterature vision is often described as the desired future position or purpose of a company. A mission expresses what one does, how one runs its business and how one will achieve the vision or fulfil its purpose. Don't get too bogged down into mission and vision statements. People are often confused about all those definitions, and even experts don't always seem to agree. Just keep it simple and use purpose to explain why you exist.

Having worked with many organisations, both starting and established, we broke the North Star into four core elements.

Purpose, ambitions, value and culture are all tied together. Knowing what you stand for, what you aspire to, what value you bring and how you will work together enables success, even in turbulent times.

A. PURPOSE

Why do you exist?

B. AMBITIONS

What does future success look like?

C. VALUE

What value do you want to create for your stakeholders?

D. CULTURE

What culture do you need to succeed?
What behaviours and mindset will you need?

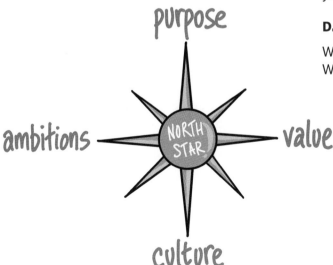

> "Ask yourself where it is you want to go... It is often said that life is a journey. But sometimes it's hard to know which path to follow when signs point in so many directions. Take a moment to slow down to a more thoughtful pace, to ponder, reflect, imagine, and envision."
> — Peter H. Reynolds, The North Star

We were inspired by the bedtime story The North Star by Peter H. Reynolds[8]. It's a beautifully illustrated book inspiring people to observe, to wonder and to consider diverging from the well-worn path – to follow their dreams. And following your dreams is exactly what you need to do to find your true North. It's the reason you exist, your "raison d'être".

Reflecting on your future North Star is the perfect moment to dream big together. With your eyes wide open so you see the possibilities, explore your way forward off the beaten path.

Your North Star is something that will help you for years to come. Purpose and culture will probably not change rapidly, but your ambitions and the value you deliver may need to be revised more regularly.

We therefore recommend you revisit your ambitions and value on a yearly basis or whenever the conditions around you have changed dramatically.

A. PURPOSE

Let's start with purpose

Why do you exist? What is your identity? Why do you do what you do?

Defining your why is not easy. You need to capture the minds and hearts of people you can do business with and attract those who share the same beliefs. Most often when you define your why, it becomes easier to find your how and your what. This applies to individuals as well as businesses. Individuals will create their own purpose, but it is the role of an organisation to build the company's purpose while helping individuals find their individual purpose. When those two connect you release energy, sparks of inspiration.

As a business you must try to find an authentic purpose that inspires people. This should help you find the reasons your company does what it does. If you see you can't fulfil your purpose, you may need to start doing things differently or even transform your company (or yourself). It's also possible you need to rethink your purpose or adjust it. But always make sure it is inspiring and meaningful to everyone on board.

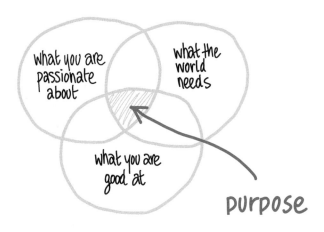

Individuals will create their own purpose, but it is the role of an organisation to build the company's purpose while helping individuals find their individual purpose.

> "Let's discuss why a company exists in the first place. In other words why we are here? We have to go deeper and find the real reasons for our being. Whereas you might achieve a goal or complete a strategy, you cannot fulfill a purpose; it's like a guiding star on the horizon—forever pursued but never reached."[9]
> — David Packard, co-founder of Hewlett-Packard

Your purpose should describe your reason for being and the positive impact your organisation wants to have in the world and on society. It lies at the intersection of what you are passionate about, what the world needs and what you have to offer. If it is compelling enough, people feel they're part of something that serves a bigger purpose. This is not about making money or pursuing profits, but about finding the driving force for achieving them.

We would like to point out the difference between "destination" and "direction of travel". Stephen Quest, the Director-General of the Joint Research Centre of the European Commission, whom we worked with for over two years told us the following: "One of the issues we faced with 'selling' the North Star to our scientists was that quite a few of them took it literally: 'you are literally asking us to go to the North Star and I don't want to, I like planet Earth…'. So, I found myself being very precise in saying we were (just) fixing a direction of travel for our journey, rather than a fixed destination (too rigid, in my view, anyway), and that the function of the North Star was to guide us towards that direction of travel." This is coherent with the Hewlett-Packard quote above.

In December 2021, Adam Bryant, author and managing director of The ExCo Group, wrote in a blogpost that employees are demanding that their work, and their employers, stand for something. This is in part the result of the shift from shareholder to stakeholder capitalism. He added that the pandemic made many people reflect more on the "why" of their jobs. This purpose feels unique to the company, there are facts and details to support it by showing what it looks like in action, and all employees can have a sense of how they are contributing directly to something that is bigger than the company itself. 'That is the purpose of purpose.'[10]

Simon Sinek says: "People don't buy what you do, they buy [because of] why you do it."[11] The same accounts for people joining or leaving your organisation or company.

'Why' is probably the most important message that an organisation or individual can communicate as this is what inspires others to action.

According to E&Y, purpose driven companies outperform the marketplace by 42%.[12]

But how do you create your own purpose? Can you co-create it? We believe it can be done on the company level, division level or for strategic cross-team initiatives, and even on the individual level. The same principles apply for all.

When you do a quick search on the internet for tools or templates to create purpose statements, you'll find plenty of suggestions. Many of them, however, are focused on goal setting. For purpose we find that too complicated. It's too much of the head, not enough of the heart. So, for those who like tools or templates, we share two visual approaches of our own. Feel free to experiment, add or remove elements.

TOOL
CO-CREATING YOUR PURPOSE

Step 1: Brainstorm why you exist as a team

- ☑ Reflect on the 'Why do we exist?' question.

- ☑ Write down words or short sentences (think in taglines) that come to mind (use sticky notes and stick them on a board).

- ☑ When done cluster similar ideas. Spot the big categories.

Step 2: Have an open discussion.

- ☑ Go through the clustered categories.

- ☑ Observe how people react to the clusters, words or sentences.

- ☑ Feel where the energy level is going. What excites them the most?

Step 3: Converge into draft purpose statements.

- ☑ Formulate two to three draft versions of the purpose, like inspiring taglines.

- ☑ Write those drafts on a flipchart so everyone can see them. Use the template on the next page.

- ☑ Let it sink in. Then take a break. Maybe even sleep on it. Finalise the tagline that sounds right. Make sure it resonates with people inside and outside your organisation.

TOOL
PURPOSE IN A SENTENCE

Step 1: Stick the template on a wall or flipchart

Write down the answers to the following questions. One answer per sticky note.

☑ How you do what you do.
☑ Why you do what you do.
☑ Who you do it for.

Step 2: Stick the answers in the right category.

☑ If you've done this well, you'll have a few options on the wall.

☑ Try to form a sentence combining the elements.

☑ If it sounds better with only or two elements, go for it. Just make sure it answers the question why you do what you do.

Step 3: Form a sentence combining the elements.

☑ Agree where the sticky notes belong.

☑ Make sure all elements have sticky notes.

☑ Rephrase where you feel it's needed.

how we do
what we do

why we do
what we do

who we do
it for

INDUSTRY E

"Spreading the power of optimism."

Life is Good

"Create the beauty that moves the world."

L'Oreal

"Make a contribution to the world by making tools for the mind that advance humankind."

Apple's purpose of 1980's

"To improve people's health and well-being through meaningful innovation."

Philips

"Bringing our heart to every moment of your health."

CVSHealth

"Accelerate the world's transition to sustainable energy and autonomy."

Tesla

KAMPLES

"Make all chocolate 100% slave-free across the globe."

Tony Chocoloney

"To educate the citizens and citizen-leaders for our society."

Harvard University

"We're in business to save home planet."

Patagonia

"Inspire and build the builders of tomorrow."

Lego

"Empower every person and every organisation on the planet to achieve more."

Microsoft

"To organise the world's information and make it universally accessible and useful."

Google

"Advance the way people live and work."

Hewlett Packard Enterprise (created in 2014)

EXAMPLES CO-CREATION

Swoove Studio, Intelligent Internet Machines
3D animation startup

SES
Global leading satellite operator

purpose

JRC provides independent evidence-based knowledge & science supporting EU policies to positively impact society

Joint Research Centre (JRC)
European Commission

making everyone shine no easy basket on & around the court

Filou Oostende
Belgian basketball team

How to bring the purpose to life:

☑ Set the context: explain the why and what of purpose and share the journey you went through.

☑ Get everyone aligned on our new purpose: ask them "What words come to mind when you read the purpose?" and "What will our main stakeholders say, if we realise our purpose. (e.g. employees, customers and society)?"

☑ Activate your purpose: co-create in workshops around "What must happen to bring our purpose to life?" List desired actions and initiatives for your internal and external stakeholders.

☑ Take all inputs and leverage this in your action plan (you'll need this later).

B. AMBITIONS

Now you know your purpose, you need to set your ambitions. On top of your direction of travel and your purpose, your ambitions provide desired points of destination for the organisation, helping to focus efforts and resources on achieving specific objectives. They could be seen as waypoints, places to stop on your journey.

What does future success look like? What is it you want to achieve?

Defining future success will help align the efforts of different teams and departments within the organisation. Finding common goals is important for team cohesion. Making sure these goals are ambitious is important. If you don't stretch yourself, you will deliver less. They also serve as a motivator for employees, making them participate in the organisation's success. Ambitions can also cover different time horizons. They could be medium to long term as the conditions you operate in can force you to change.

Ambitions will inform the plan, which we call the Bridge as explained in Chapter 4.

TOOL
CO-CREATING YOUR AMBITIONS

Step 1: Brainstorm around the big dreams and ambitious goals

- ☑ Imagine you're in the future. Describe what success looks like. In total five or six lines.

- ☑ Make sure it's future things, things you don't have yet. These are your ambitions.

- ☑ Make it human. Make it personal.

Step 2: Visually facilitate the convergence

- ☑ Paraphrase what the group says, so it is short, snappy and easy to remember.

- ☑ Always look for consensus.

- ☑ Stop when the group starts repeating or rephrasing what is already on the board.

Step 3: Look at the harvest

- ☑ Take a step back and look at what you've co-created. Read out loud what you've written down.

- ☑ Don't overdo it. These are not KPIs.

- ☑ See if you missed anything.

If it's a large group, you can use sticky notes and then cluster them, similar to the purpose conversation. Ideally your list is a set of ambitious goals addressing your main stakeholders.

ambitions

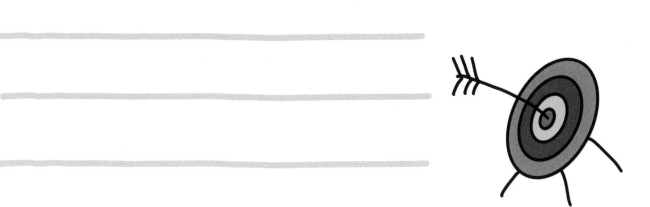

EXAMPLES CO-CREATION

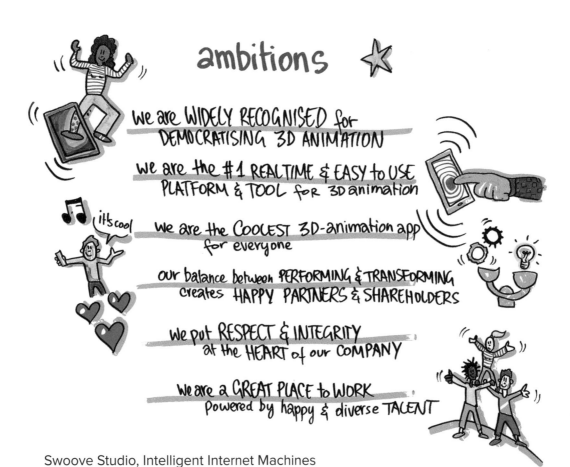

ambitions

We are WIDELY RECOGNISED for DEMOCRATISING 3D ANIMATION

We are the #1 REALTIME & EASY to USE PLATFORM & TOOL for 3D animation

We are the COOLEST 3D-animation app for everyone

it's cool

Our balance between PERFORMING & TRANSFORMING creates HAPPY PARTNERS & SHAREHOLDERS

We put RESPECT & INTEGRITY at the HEART of our COMPANY

We are a GREAT PLACE to WORK Powered by happy & diverse TALENT

Swoove Studio, Intelligent Internet Machines
3D animation startup

AMBITIONS

we believe in CONTENT & CONNECTIVITY everywhere

we are the leading cloud-enabled satellite based INTELLIGENT CONNECTIVITY provider

we are FUTURE PROOF powered by SUSTAINABLE GROWTH & INNOVATION

we are passionate about CUSTOMER EXPERIENCE & focused on CUSTOMER SUCCESS

SES is a GREAT PLACE to WORK

We are here to MAKE a DIFFERENCE

SES
Global leading satellite operator

C. VALUE

Imagine you have reached success. What do you get in return?

What value will you create for your stakeholders in the future? What is the impact you'll have on your stakeholders?

To our surprise many organisations don't often reflect on the true value or benefits they want to create for their stakeholders. And stakeholders should include anyone impacted by your success or your failures today and tomorrow. So think customers, employees, partners, suppliers, society, planet, shareholders, board, leadership, etc.

For each stakeholder you've got a series of areas you'll be impacting, things that might go up like profit, fun, quality, revenue, and things that may go down like risk, waste, losses, carbon footprint, etc.

These value areas are your measures of success. When you do this right, some can be used to build your key performance indicators (KPI).

IMAGINE YOU HAVE REACHED SUCCESS. WHAT DO YOU GET IN RETURN? WHAT IS THE TRUE VALUE YOU WILL CREATE FOR YOUR STAKEHOLDERS?

TOOL
CO-CREATING YOUR VALUE

Step 1: Brainstorm around the stakeholder groups

- ☑ List the big stakeholders. Think external and internal.

- ☑ When complete you should have a clear list of stakeholders and areas of impact.

- ☑ Try to limit it to four to six stakeholders. Merge if you have more.

Step 2: Determine the value for each of your stakeholders

- ☑ Per stakeholder, describe the value you will be creating in the future.

- ☑ For each value, think of the impact of your success: what will increase, what will decrease?

- ☑ Aim for five to ten per stakeholder.

value

EXAMPLES CO-CREATION

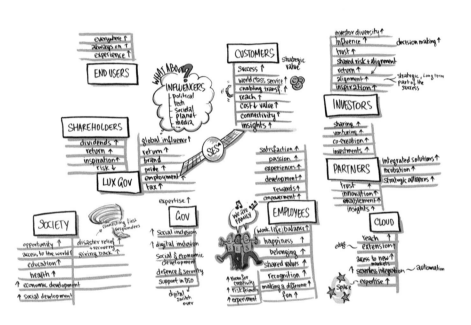

SES
Global leading satellite operator

Joint Research Centre (JRC)
European Commission

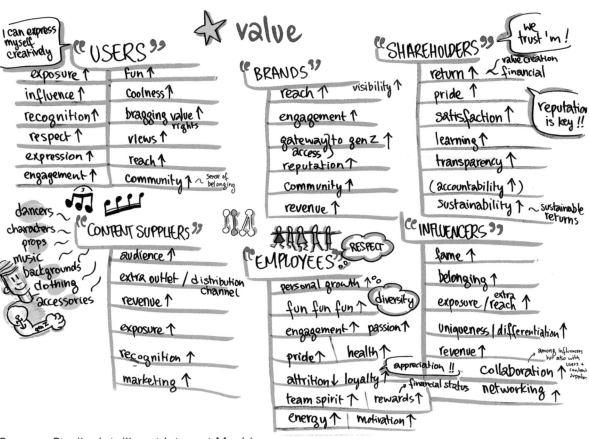

Swoove Studio, Intelligent Internet Machines
3D animation startup

D. CULTURE

Purpose is what drives you. Ambitions are the goals. But culture defines how you behave, how you will get there.

What culture do you need to succeed? What behaviours and mindset enable that culture?

Culture is the backbone of your organisation. Culture includes values and norms. Culture is how you sell, how you deliver, how you communicate, how you recruit. Culture impacts your reputation. Many books and posts have been written about the importance of culture and how it relates to succeeding in business. Seventy per cent of transformations fail, largely due to people- and culture-related challenges.[13] But why is it so hard to create a successful culture and why is it so critical in the workplace.

Culture encompasses customs and social behaviour of a particular group of people or society. This also exists at company level. In a company culture drives how people work and interact. It reflects the beliefs, ideologies, backgrounds and practices of an organisation. Culture is dynamic, not static and changes over time in small, subtle ways.

Culture is also about how it feels to work with us, to work for us, to buy from us. It is what creates experiences, so-called moments of truth. If your employees aren't speaking up, you probably need to blame the company culture.[14] A strong culture creates stickiness. It creates loyal employees and loyal customers. Culture trumps strategy any day. Or more vividly "Culture eats strategy for breakfast".[15]

Culture can be explicit, as in very visible and defined, or implicit, as in ingrained in the company, lived by the employees. Taking a fresh look at the values and behaviours that shape a day in a life of your company and see what you need to succeed in the future will help you to unleash the right energy for the transformation at hand.

If you want to become more transformative and innovative, culture is the hardest bit to change. Re-culturing your organisation is as important as reimagining other parts of your business.

Defining your desired culture is the first step as covered below. Activating and living your culture needs time to sink in and needs perseverance. Behaviours must change. Culture transformation is the biggest and the hardest step to get right. As shown in Chapter 9 to succeed in your culture transformation you will need to work on Heartset, Mindset and Actionset.

The tool on the next page focuses on answering the following questions: what culture (values/norms) do we need to succeed? What do we keep and what do we need to develop? What behaviours and mindset support that culture?

TOOL
CO-CREATING YOUR CULTURE

Step 1: Ideate the values, characteristics, and norms

- ☑ Put aside your existing culture and start with a blank canvas answering what values, characteristics or norms you need to be successful (think ambitions and value).

- ☑ Write down the values you believe are essential to your company's success. (One value per sticky notes and stick them on a board.)

- ☑ Cluster them into six to eight groups and name them.

Step 2: Visually facilitate the convergence

- ☑ If you have a documented culture or values and norms, review them and see if you missed any critical ones. If they are truly lived, they should already pop up in step 1.

- ☑ Check if the wording is simple and understandable for everyone, easy to remember.

- ☑ Avoid semantic discussions. Keep the end in mind.

Step 3: Describe the behaviours

- ☑ Draft a set (three to max five) of expected behavioural patterns and habits per value, so everyone understands what you mean and what behaviour is expected.

- ☑ Put it all on one chart.

- ☑ Make it visual.

culture

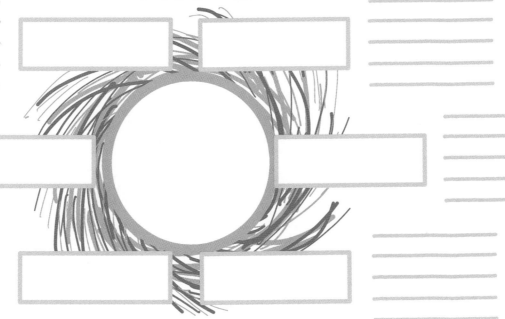

EXAMPLES VALUES, CHARACTERISTIC

We've added a list for inspiration. It's non-exhaustive, but it can help you if you need it.
Do not show this list. Just use at the end of step 1 to see if you missed anything.

Professional	Attention for details
Accountable (keeping promises)	Transparent & Discrete
Fair	One Company
Personal growth	Respectful
Trust	Trustworthy
Innovative	Integer
Entrepreneurial	Ethical
Edgy and Cool	Authentic
Pioneer	Appetite for exploration
Meticulous	Passionate

D NORMS

Curious

Open minded

Growth Mindset

Collaborative

Agile

Flexible

Vulnerable

Diverse & Inclusive

Making a difference

Customer centric

Result-driven

ROI-driven

Empathetic

Fact based (Data-driven) decision making

Run by ideas, not hierarchy

Fun

Impactful

EXAMPLES BEHAVIOURS

Innovative

"We recognise that success requires experimentation, rapid iteration, and learning from failure."

"We value creative ability and curiosity more than just experience in our talent sourcing."

"We empower people to take considered risks and seek needed resources."

Trust

"We do as we say."

"We listen attentively, speak candidly, treat others respectfully and criticise constructively."

"We have each other's back."

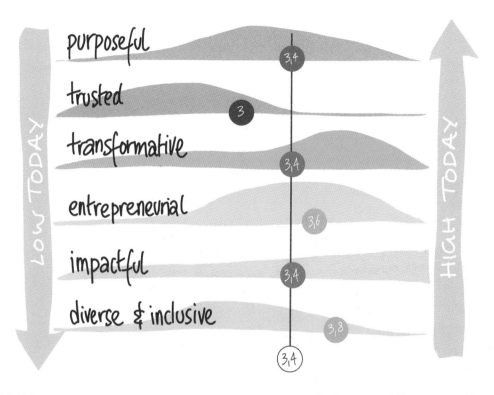

Validate and rate

☑ After tweaking and tuning the culture and behaviours, finalise the list.

☑ Rate each of them on weak today or strong today (one to five) using manual dot-voting or digital polling systems e.g Mentimeter, slido.[16]

Activate and live your culture

☑ Defining your culture is one thing. Activating and living your culture is another. It is the hardest.

☑ In Chapter 9 about Heartset, Mindset and Actionset we'll hand you a practical framework to activate and transform your culture.

EXAMPLES CO-CREATION

culture

we exhibit the right behaviour

respect
we care for eachother, ourselves, society
we trust eachother

openness
we are diverse & inclusive
we challenge ourselves

opinions
people
age...
geography...

we got your back...

CRD

innovation
we are brave, bold, daring
we are inspiring
we are allowed to take risk

commitment
we are result driven
we excel in what we do
& we are passionate about it

teamwork
we collaborate beyond siloes
we partner with the outside world
we empower people to be their best self

co-create

Corporate Research & Development (CRD) Umicore
Leading circular materials technology company

trust
integrity
transparent

innovative
open-minded
cocreative

engaged
passionate

culture

Connecting
the dots
Sense-making
sharing

Collaborative
inclusive
empowered

excellent
ethical
accountable

TRANSPARENCY

CUSTOMER
centricity

TRUST

INTEGRITY

INNOVATIVE

COURAGEOUS

ENTREPRENEURIAL

IN IT
TOGETHER

AGILE

INCLUSIVE

MAKING
a DIFFERENCE

PROUD to be
HERE

impact

GROWTH MINDSET

YES AND...
mindset

Joint Research Centre (JRC)
European Commission

SES
Global leading satellite operator

2.4 WRAPPING THE NORTH STAR

What will the stakeholders say when we reach success?

You know you made it when your stakeholders say so. A great way to end the North Star exercise is to ask your team to empathise with your stakeholders (e.g. press, employees, customers, partners) and think about what they will say in the future when you successfully deliver on your North Star. You ask them to think in quotes: things people might actually say when asked on the spot, rather than lengthy boring phrases.

Swoove Studio, Intelligent Internet Machines
3D animation startup

Telecommunications & Integrated Applications (TIA)
European Space Agency

TOOL
STAKEHOLDER EXPERIENCE

☑ Gather in small groups.

☑ Brainstorm about what stakeholders will say in the future when you reach success.

☑ Select the best and fill out the template.

☑ Aim for 2 or 3 per stakeholder. Just take the biggest stakeholders.

what will our stakeholders say ?

What you have learned...

A North Star serves as a compass and drives everyone towards a common direction.

To find it you answer four key questions:

- ☑ **Purpose:** why do you exist ?
- ☑ **Ambitions:** what does your future success look like?
- ☑ **Value:** what value do you want to create for your stakeholders?
- ☑ **Culture:** what culture will help you get there?

The material you have co-created on your North Star can be displayed in your office and can be used for your marketing and branding purposes.

We recommend you revisit your ambitions and value on a yearly basis or whenever the conditions around you have changed dramatically.

CHAPTER 3
THE CURRENT REALITY

Where are you today?

What you will learn in this chapter...

In the previous chapter we looked at how asking the right Power Question can do miracles and how you can imagine your North Star.

This section dives deeper into the various challenges and opportunities you are facing. What trends you see and what they mean for you.

CHAPTER IN BRIEF

THE POWER QUESTION

Where are we today?

THE PROBLEM

Teams like to dive quickly into solving problems.

They do not always see what is truly happening inside and outside the company.

Often leadership teams delegate the analysis of the current state to a small group or even an outside party to prepare the transformation plans but fail to tap into their own group intelligence.

THE SOLUTION

Facilitate a brainstorm on what you see happening inside and outside the company that can help us or block our future success.

THE REWARD

A clear, aligned and co-created picture of the biggest trends, challenges and opportunities, from the inside-out as well as from the outside-in.

3.1 YOUR STARTING POSITION

Knowing what can block or enable future scenarios of success is critical. This implies you know where you're going. You could dive straight into the current reality and write down all you know, but just like with travelling, it might be wise to first decide where you're going or what you are travelling for.

"If you don't know where you're going, you're usually going nowhere!"

– the Cheshire Cat in Alice in Wonderland by Lewis Carroll.

outside-in   what do we see?   inside-out

trends   blockers   enablers

Start making sense

To be able to Transform while Performing you will need to understand today's reality and contrast it with what it might look like tomorrow. You need to see and sense the big picture and understand the impact it can have on you and your surroundings. Becoming a sensemaker[17] will put you one or more steps ahead of the pack. A sensemaker understands today's reality and sees the implications in the near future. This helps you make sense of the complexity in an ever-changing world, connect the dots and translate it. Sensemakers need to help people understand the world without overwhelming them and get them energised even if the future sky might look gloomy. This is a trait many leaders will need to develop to be able to Transform while Performing.

Most people see the bigger trends and sense what's happening in the world. They're reading articles written by experts and futurologists and are following change makers. And they feel the immediate implications on their businesses. But seeing and sensing is one thing, changing the course is something else. Most lack insight into how they can move the needle and transform their established organisation so that it takes radically different actions, addresses market shifts and grasps emerging opportunities. Many people vastly underestimate the speed of change and its impact.

Taking a critical look at yourself, and your organisation, from various angles will generate critical insights into trends and what can block or enable your future success. It helps you see what others don't see or perhaps don't even want to see. You make sense out of the complexity around you and what this could mean to you, to your people and to your business. It will definitely not provide an answer to all your problems, but it certainly puts you on the way.

Let's deep dive into your current reality, to understand your starting position and gain insights into trends and potential road blockers on the way to your destination. But this conversation is not only about the stuff that doesn't work. It's important to also look at what you already have that works well, that you can build on. An open and honest conversation on your current reality should give you a solid overview of what works and what doesn't in your current way of working. Some excellent facilitators we worked with called it the good, the bad and the ugly conversation.

A. Look at the megatrends

Megatrends are powerful, transformative forces that could change the global economy, business and society. The forces that could be changing the way we have lived for centuries. We are looking at five to ten years from now, at trends that most likely will have a global impact and have a disruptive market potential. Major categories include climate change, demographic and societal evolutions, shifts in economic or political power, technological evolutions, resource scarcity, medical and scientific changes.

Seeing and understanding those global economic, business and societal megatrends, will help you to anticipate change and gain critical insights needed to create options to respond.

The internet offers tons of research, data, and predictions from sources like data scientists, futurists, experts, think tanks, independent international organisations and consulting firms. Also ask openAI tools like ChatGPT[18] and see what data they can pull. Take some time to scan some of these and try not to get lost by checking the sources, comparing and sharing with co-workers.

B. Outside-in versus inside-out

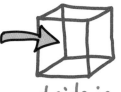

outside-in   inside-out

When reflecting on your current reality, it is good to combine inside-out with outside-in views.

A lot of organisations tend to look at things from the inside-out. That's fine because that's what you have under your control. And it's where the change will need to happen. From the inside-out. Inside-out views are about employees, leadership, culture, operations, innovation, etc.

The outside-in on the other hand include megatrends, economy, market changes, politics, competition, etc. Views can be taken from your research around megatrends and trends specific to your industry. But outside-in can also relate to looking at your immediate ecosystem, with clients or partners, and empathise with what they are facing. Outside-in thinking can inspire you to do things differently.

All these views can be distilled from surveys and research, but also simply by asking the various players in the ecosystem. When planning your transformation it pays off to interview a few of these clients or partners, or citizens if you're working for a government administration, and check what they have to say about you. Try to connect the dots between the outside-in and the inside-out views, if any. Are there conflicting views? Can you spot patterns?

Lastly, to prepare for next steps, you could prioritise and shortlist the scenarios that are most likely to happen or are most desirable. There are useful exercises that you can run to anticipate these and create options. This will allow you to take adequate strategic decisions, quantifying impact and prioritising investments. We will not elaborate on the scientific approach further, but focus on what you can do with a group of people in the room, tapping into the collective human intelligence.

Putting this research and the insights together, ideally prior to this exercise, allows you to challenge the status quo and start acting on the present to create your own future.

3.2 HOW DO YOU TAKE A SNAPSHOT OF YOUR CURRENT REALITY?

So how do you structure a conversation to gain critical insights into your current reality? Start by asking the following question:

What in our current reality can block or enable future success?

You will quickly notice this is usually an easy conversation. Here we are looking for what-elements, not so much why nor how.

It's in most people's comfort zone to talk about the problems and challenges they face every day. It's usually not that easy to see opportunities and some people might forget to mention what works well, what strengths you must build on. Make sure that you cover positives and negatives. The negatives might be hard to change, but could be critical. The positive ones might catalyse change. You will also spot things that are easy to fix, the so-called low hanging fruit.

Some tips for this exercise:

Do research upfront.
Look at megatrends. Interview key stakeholders. Analyse available data. And put it all together on a knowledge wall. Now step back and try to gain insights from all this research. How aligned is your research? Do you spot patterns or big themes? Are there any blind spots. Things you don't know. This helps you formulate questions for your next steps.

Boost co-creation making visual notes.
A tip for the notetaker is to not just capture bullets and words, like agility or culture, but write down short statements that that will help you remember what it was about. For instance, 'we lack agility at our front desk', or 'we don't have a true sales culture'. We insist on working visually, because it helps the group keep track of what was already said. This helps the co-creation. Participants trigger each other which provides a very natural flow of the conversation. Honour the conversation. Don't write down the first thing they shout. Write it down when you feel there is consensus.

117

This is a diverging conversation.
Anything that comes to mind related to your current reality is a candidate to be put on the wall. We are looking for actionable insights. Try not to go too much into detail, stay away from problem-solving. We'll get there later.

As a last step look at the wall and compare it with what you learned from the preparation and research you did before the session.

"We don't see things as they are, we see them as we are."
– Anais Nin.

Many have told us: "this is like group therapy!" It kind of is. By framing the conversation, creating a safe environment, facilitating open dialogue, and listening to each other, you gradually generate critical insights into your current reality. This is where you create awareness. This is where you plant the seeds for change.

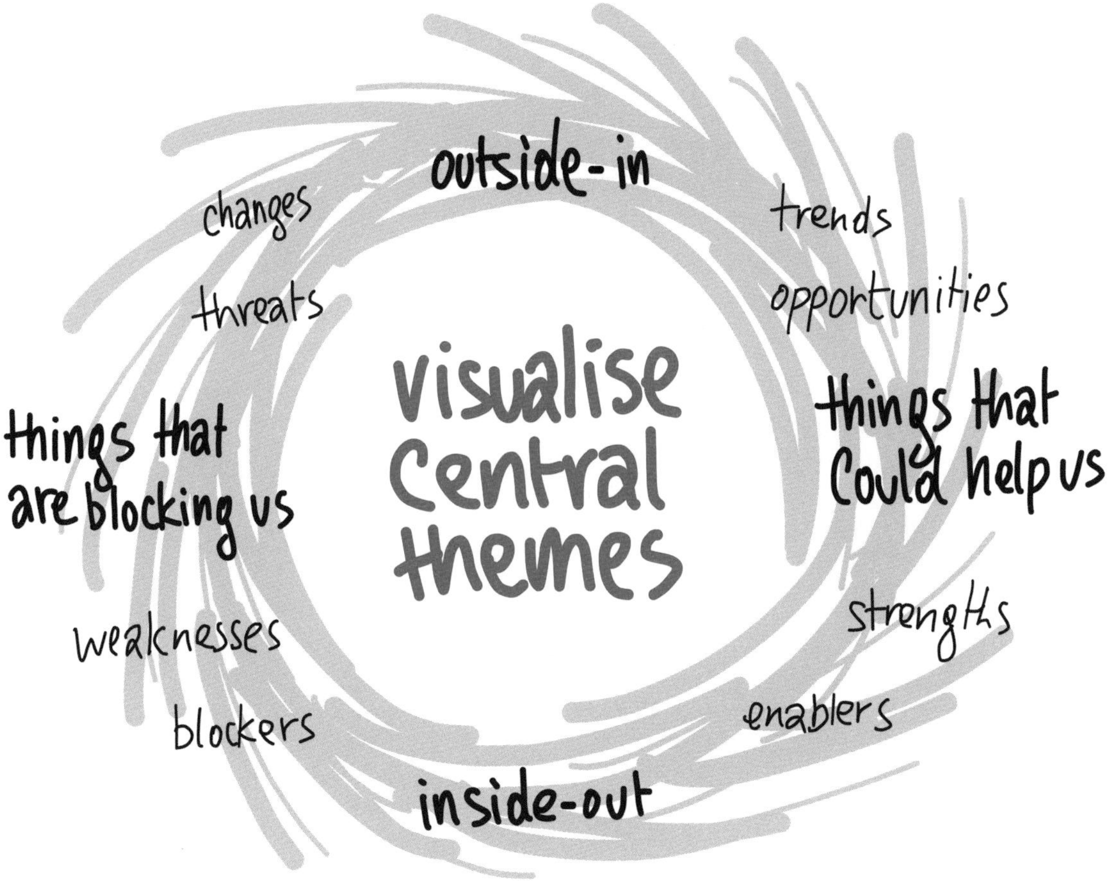

outside-in

changes

trends

threats

opportunities

things that
are blocking us

visualise
central
themes

things that
could help us

weaknesses

strengths

blockers

enablers

inside-out

TOOL
GAIN INSIGHTS INTO YOUR CURRENT REALITY

☑ Look at what you have already created during the Power Question and North Star conversations.

☑ Brainstorm around what in your current reality could block or enable future success.

☑ List megatrends and evaluate how they impact your current reality.

☑ Cover both inside-out and outside-in.

☑ Capture key insights on a new flipchart or whiteboard.

For groups of less than twenty you can easily do this in a plenary setting. For larger groups, you may need to split them up, use Post-its or online collaboration tools.

current reality

trend 1

trend 2

blockers

trend 3

...

outside-in

enablers

inside-out

EXAMPLES CO-CREATION

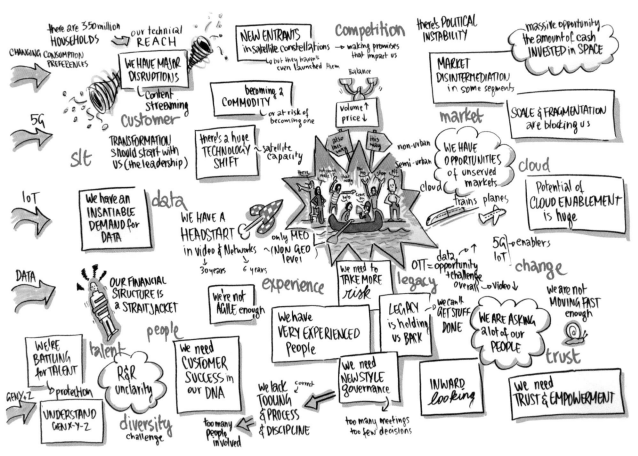

SES
Global leading satellite operator

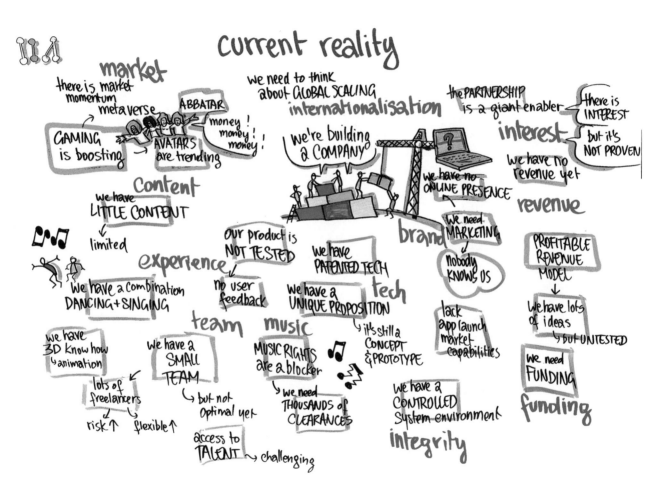

current reality

Swoove Studio, Intelligent Internet Machines
3D animation startup

What you have learned...

☑ **Actionable insights:** You've learned to run a deep dive into your current reality, looking for insights that will be helpful for building the actions. When done well, the wall should reflect the good (do more of), the bad and the ugly of an organisation related to the challenges and outcomes described in the Power Question.

☑ **Trends, blockers and enablers:** You've aligned your teams on the trends, challenges and opportunities to your future success.

☑ **Outside-in and inside-out:** It should show what's happening on the outside, and what's happening on the inside. It should show what works, what doesn't and what is missing. Anticipation starts with seeing and knowing what is happening around you, looking at the larger picture with an open mind.

You know what to work on next to be able to reach success.
How you will build the bridge from your current state to your future state is what we'll cover in the next chapter.

PART II GET EVERYONE TO ACT

CHAPTER 4
THE BRIDGE

How do you get there?

What you will learn in this chapter...

In the previous chapters we looked at your current reality, and we showed you how you can craft your future North Star. In this chapter we build the bridge that connects your current state to your future world.

We'll look at the strategic initiatives and concrete next steps that you need to realise your North Star.

CHAPTER IN BRIEF

THE POWER QUESTION

How do you get there?

THE PROBLEM

Action plans often are either too fluffy or too detailed.

You want plans that are addressing your current state focused on the North Star, with enough level of detail to make them actionable and impactful.

THE SOLUTION

Build the Bridge using the why/ what/how technique, breaking it down into strategic themes and initiatives in line with the North Star.

THE REWARD

You'll get a strong action plan, that addresses your Power Question, your current reality and paves the way towards your North Star.

4.1 CONNECT THE CURRENT TO THE FUTURE WORLD

Now that you know what it is you aspire to (Chapter 2 The North Star), it's time to plan some action.

How do you get there? How do you build the Bridge between the current and the future state?

We'll answer the Power Question by breaking it down into strategic themes and initiatives. This is where you draft your strategic plan. This is how you start making change. This is how you get to action following your North Star.

If you followed the steps the previous chapters, by now you've done the following:

- You've agreed on your Power Question, listing the big problem(s) you need to solve (Chapter 1).

- You have aligned as a group on what success looks like, your future, desired state, and you've found your North Star (Chapter 2), your guiding compass.

- You've drafted a bigger purpose for your organisation and listed a set of ambitions. You've also been exploring the ecosystem, with the value you'll be creating in the future for all your stakeholders. And you'll also have had a deep conversation on the ideal culture you need.

- You've also taken a critical look at your current reality, your starting position (Chapter 3), which gave you a good overview of what you see happening inside and outside your organisation, what works and what doesn't.

So, in short, you have a good view on where you are and where you are going, but you still need a map to get there.

This visual shows where you are in the process.

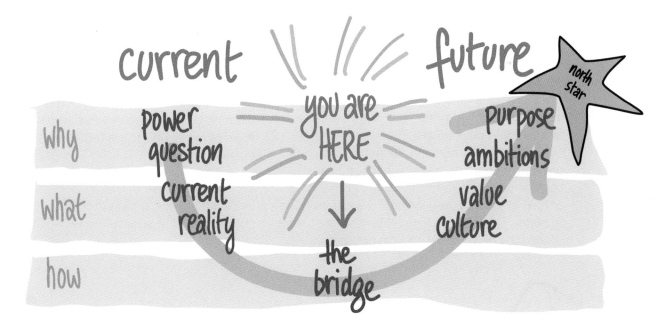

All this is valuable input to ponder the big themes of your transformation plan. To start building the bridge between current and future. The plan of action that describes what you are going to do and how you are going to execute.

There's a variety of ways to do this, and we'll dive right into it. But before let's remind ourselves of the problem we are trying to fix with this section.

How do we build a Bridge between the current and the future state to follow your North Star?

We've seen quite a few transformation plans that lack goals or even miss a sense of purpose, making them just endless lists of actions and initiatives. Even people who were involved in creating the action plan and put their name to a particular action have sometimes forgotten what that action was for and what (part of the) problem it was intending to solve. Therefore, it is important to keep track of the why of each action or initiative, before detailing the what and the how. In this chapter we'll show you a few techniques to keep line of sight and not get lost in the detail when you enter the actual action phase.

On the other hand, you also want to avoid plans that lack detail and are too fluffy to make any impact. In one of our workshops a participant wrote down in the action plan that it was necessary to "operationalise the action plan". In such a case you should ask the person what he or she meant by that and get that level of detail on the wall. Otherwise, it will be wasted on you.

We call this phase in the process the Bridge, because it is the bridge that connects your current world to your future world. It bridges

Too detailed	Just right	Too fluffy
• Jumps straight into action	• Every action contains a brief why, what and how, specifying "what the action is", "why is it needed", "how do you plan to kick it off"	• Too high level
• Very technical		• Not concrete enough
• Lacks focus on user or customer		• Not actionable
• Only focused on the mind, not on the heart (e.g. setting up a tool instead of creating an excellent experience)	• You may add who owns the action, who needs to be involved, when it has to be finished or kicked off, etc.	• Too focused on the heart, not enough on the mind
	• Balancing the heart and mind	
Too detailed example: Fix VPC Automation to Market Parity	*Right example: organise participative all employee event to update everyone on our renewed ambitions*	*Fluffy example: scale innovation*

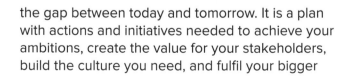

the gap between today and tomorrow. It is a plan with actions and initiatives needed to achieve your ambitions, create the value for your stakeholders, build the culture you need, and fulfil your bigger purpose. It is the plan you need to find success, your North Star. But it requires you to stay alert when you're building it and be inspired by what you've created so far.

4.2 BUILDING YOUR BRIDGE

So we all agree it's time to get things done. You'll need to come up with the right actions and divide the work. A very powerful way of doing this is by making use of the why-what-how technique.

On the next pages you'll get various suggestions on how you can build it up visually.

When you complete this exercise, you'll have a strong action plan that is aligned with your why (North Star) and addresses your what (Power Question and current reality). It will be a holistic plan, from problems to outcomes, from current to future, with a clear set of themes and detailed actions needed to kick-start the transformation. By no means we promise that this will be final, nor will it be complete, but it will be a good enough plan to start working on. A plan for a plan. A first step, figuring out what is needed for the next iteration.

It's a journey

Iterate and fine-tune the Bridge to

☑ amplify the work

☑ multiply the effect by spreading it throughout the organisation

☑ increase buy-in.

Before you know it, it will become self-perpetuating habit, and everybody will be in on it. And the ones who aren't will need to speak up. You can't leave anyone behind. At some point everyone joining the journey will need to cross the Bridge. Transformers and performers.

A NORTH STAR WITHOUT ACTION IS A DREAM, ACTION WITHOUT A NORTH STAR IS A NIGHTMARE

Adapted from a Japanse proverb[19]

TOOL
CO-CREATING YOUR BRIDGE

Step 1: Find the big themes

☑ Look at the visual output of the Power Question, Current Reality, Ambitions and Value.

☑ Distil five to six big themes.

☑ When done, ask yourself: *are they truly helping to achieve our ambitions?* If the answer is no, rephrase until you get it right.

Step 2: Write down initiatives per theme

☑ Take a flipchart per theme and list the initiatives needed to make it happen.

☑ Reflect on the why/what/how of each theme. Repeat for each theme.

☑ Summarise on one chart. Try to keep it simple. Leave space for people to breathe and let them fill in the how.

bridge

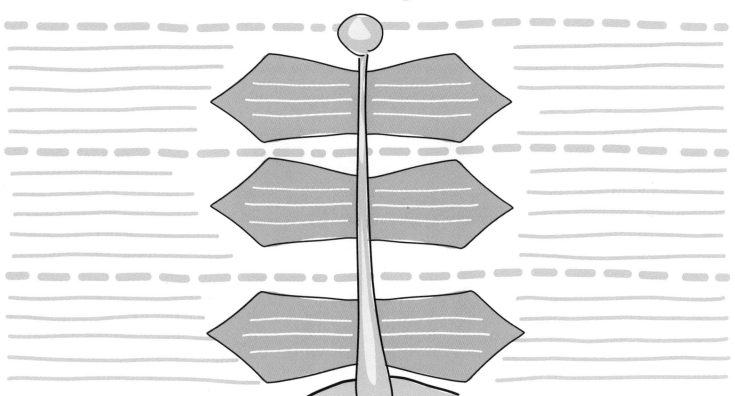

FLIPCHART STRUCTURE

	THEME NAME Name the theme or topic	**EXAMPLE** Excellent in-store customer experiences
WHY should we care?	• Why should we do this? • Why is this important for you?	• We want our customers to feel welcome and at ease when they walk into our stores. • When our customers feel at ease they will buy more and come back more. • This is part of our values.
WHAT is required to be successful?	• What can enable or block our success? • What do we need to succeed? • What are the critical success factors? • Write down what has to happen to reach the desired state.	• Our staff is very accommodating and welcoming to our guests without being pushy. • We have an intuitive store layout, allowing people to easily find what they are looking for. • Throughout our stores there are many happy surprises, such as a play area for kids, comfortable seating for mom or dad in a cosy corner, etc. • We have instore WIFI that is easy and fast. • Our staff are easy to find and jump right in when they see guests might need help.

	THEME NAME **Name the theme or topic**	**EXAMPLE** **Excellent in-store customer experiences**
HOW do we build the Bridge?	• What top three to five initiatives/ projects/actions should we initiate to realise this theme? • Think also about innovative ideas (at least one), not just iterative. • Anything we should stop doing? • No generic statements. Describe the action: be concise and precise. • List how you think this can be achieved.	• Redesign stores following design thinking principles. • Hire specialists to redesign the user experience. • Work with experienced staff to build checklists with relevant information and frequently asked questions. • Train store supervisors to handle incidents better. • Organise training with staff to let them reflect on what they can do to make the customer experience better. • Have a flexible and easy returns procedure.

Do this for each theme. Give yourself some time to do so. For small groups, less than 20, you can easily do this in a plenary setting. For larger teams, break up into smaller teams.

EXAMPLES BREAKOUTS

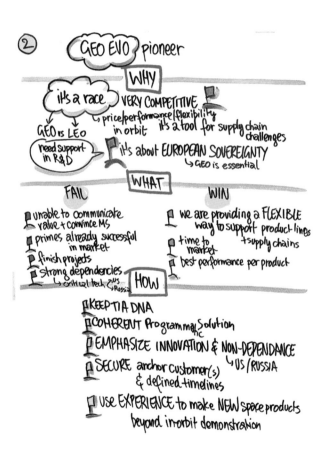

② GEO EVO pioneer

WHY

it's a race → VERY COMPETITIVE
↳ price/performance/flexibility in orbit   it's a tool for supply chain challenges

GEO vs LEO
need support in R&D   it's about EUROPEAN SOVEREIGNTY
↳ GEO is essential

WHAT

FAIL
- unable to communicate value + convince MS
- primes already successful in market
- finish projects
- strong dependencies ↳ critical tech US/Russia

WIN
- we are providing a FLEXIBLE way to support product lines + supply chains
- time to market
- best performance per product

HOW
- KEEP TIA DNA
- COHERENT Programmatic Solution
- EMPHASIZE INNOVATION & NON-DEPENDANCE ↳ US/RUSSIA
- SECURE anchor customer(s) & defined timelines
- USE EXPERIENCE to make NEW space products beyond in-orbit demonstration

Telecommunications & Integrated Applications (TIA)
European Space Agency

Break Out 3   Team: 4

WHY

1 0 4 NEEDED
- SOVEREIGNTY
- need for ~~security~~ secure communications
- crisis management & ~~climate~~ change
- Support resilience to essential services
- Long-term (beyond crisis) needs
- A cyber secure data everywhere

WHAT

Opportunities
→ Geopolitical situation
→ Political agenda (digitisation, green...)
→ Private sector leverage (legacy, commercialisation)

Threats
- EU Sec Connectivity - 4s overlap
- User Communities lack of support
- Real value not understood

HOW
- communicate & address needs of the geo opportunities
- facilitate communication between private sector & MS (ind days, webinars) demos)
- Extend applications development & legacy
- Push autonomy ↳ critical techno development

- Storytelling clarifying complementarity with Sec Conn
- storytelling clarifying value/ ROI
- User/industry days Anchor customers

Co-creation day around mental wellbeing at work.
The visual summary of some of the breakouts.

TOOL
START-STOP-CONTINUE

Quite a few of our customers felt that all these plans generated additional pressure on the teams, on top of their other work. Our advice here is to not only look at what has to be added, but also what is already ongoing and has to be (dis)continued. A start, stop, sustain exercise can be an eye-opener here. Here goes:

Start-stop-continue to optimise resources

- ☑ List all initiatives (new and ongoing).

- ☑ Evaluate what has to be started, stopped, and continued in view of the new North Star.

- ☑ Merge overlaps.

To evaluate the ongoing projects:

- ☑ Ask yourself if they are contributing to the "new" North Star and if they are performing (results vs resources).

- ☑ Decide which ones you will stop or continue.

- ☑ Evaluate impact, risks and communicate clearly to all stakeholders.

You can do this during a workshop but also as a stand-alone exercise. Doing this regularly will optimise the use of your resources, necessary to fuel your transformation.

EXAMPLES CO-CREATION

Swoove Studio, Intelligent Internet Machines
3D animation startup

what we will say after this off-site

communication

- we aligned on the why & what of our transformation
- we listed the blockers & enablers
- we brought the strategy to a wider team
- we co-created the how of our strategic plan
- we addressed the cultural aspect
- we want to get started but keep iterating the plan

Communication is always important, but especially when embarking on a transformation. This communication should include:

☑ An inspiring story around the why and what of your transformation.

☑ Clear and consistent messaging on the reasons and objectives behind the change.

☑ Clear communication channels for questions and feedback.

As you progress in the transformation, aligning, amplifying and acting, you can add:

☑ More details on the how (which you co-create with a wider group).

☑ More detailed plans and timelines.

☑ Regular updates on progress and insights.

What you have learned...

☑ **Big themes:** You've learned to cluster the transformation areas into big themes or categories and have made your teams reflect on what initiatives are needed within each theme to reach success and how it can be achieved.

☑ **Build the Bridge:** You've just learned how to close the gap between your current and your future state.

☑ **Connect the dots:** You've spotted valuable connections between different elements which will help you find your North Star.

CHAPTER 5

ALIGN, AMPLIFY AND ACT

How do you create more impact?

What you will learn in this chapter...

After the planning phase in the previous chapters, this is where the journey really begins. In this chapter we'll show you how to get everyone on board after you've created your North Star and the Bridge taking you towards the future. This is where the journey really begins. This is where you move from planning to action.

We'll show you how to make the Bridge better by involving more stakeholders and how you ensure it gets spread across the organisation. In other words how to get things done and create more impact.

CHAPTER IN BRIEF

THE POWER QUESTION

How do you get things done and create more impact?

THE PROBLEM

After creating the North Star and action plans, people often get back to their daily routines and lose momentum. Also the rest of the organisation who were not involved may not buy in which can cause the strategic action plans to have little impact.

THE SOLUTION

There's a variety of practices to align, amplify and act which will motivate people across the organisation to have more impact. Let them work out what the transformation means for them and how they can contribute to success.

THE REWARD

Get everyone on board to have lasting impact.

5.1 ALIGN, AMPLIFY AND ACT

Have you ever been in a two-day off-site where you discussed and reflected on the future of your organisation? Were you energised and excited about it and ready to take it on? Did you write your name on a board, committing to participate in some strategic actions as a next step? Can you honestly say that you followed up and executed what was agreed after the off-site? Did it have any lasting impact?

Or were you taken over by the business as usual, and not able to work on all those lovely promises made during the off-site.

A question we often get at the end of a conference or workshop is: "What do we do with all this great output?" Or: "How are we going to do all that extra work? We already have so many things to do."

One of our government clients observed this is where the journey actually begins. The planning is what we've described in the previous chapters, but this is where you start climbing the mountain. The same customer said: "Without depressing people I think it's worth underlining that this getting started is hard and can take time! In our organisation the initial resistance was the highest." We recognise that with many of our clients. That's one of the reasons we wrote this book. To offer you plenty of practical tools to address resistance and get people inspired and energised to start the journey.

5.2 HOW DO YOU CREATE MORE IMPACT? HOW DO YOU GET THINGS DONE?

157

Ed Catmull, president of Pixar and Disney Animation Studios, describes how companies often don't spend enough time nurturing and improving an initial idea and quickly produce quantity, not quality, because of the pressure to "feed the hungry beast." We also see that in the context of performing and transforming. The ideas and initiatives that came out of the strategic summit, necessary to transform the organisation, get crushed by the daily work, the pressure of performing. So, we sat around the drawing table and thought about how we could fix that problem. In most cases the solution lies in not just acting, but also aligning and amplifying.

We've created a method to align, amplify, and act. You start small with a core team to align on the key aspects of the North Star and strategy. As you progress in your transformation planning, the intention is to address a larger group of stakeholders to make the plan better and more tangible, more tactical. We call this the amplify stage. And lastly you get things done in the phase, where you multiply the effects of the transformation plan across the organisation and with your ecosystem.

Not all organisations will go through the three stages; you might jump straight to stage 2, complete all three stages or you might only undertake stage 1. You can choose to start top-down, go straight to a bottom-up approach or even both. What is important for you is to select the approach that makes the most sense for your organisation.

The 3 stages

	Align	Amplify	Act
Typical audience	**Core team** e.g. leadership team, management team, core project team, transformation lead team	**Key stakeholders, often internal, and influencers** e.g. extended leadership, managers, key stakeholders, key talent	**All other impacted** e.g. managers, experts, business units, all employees, external stakeholders
Objectives	**Aligning on the key components of the journey** • Find the North Star • Asses your current reality • Create your Bridge	**Amplifying and multiplying the impact** • Validate the North Star • Deep dive on culture and behaviours • Co-create detailed Bridge initiatives and prioritise	**Activating the plan and acting accordingly** • Implement North Star • Translate the Bridge priorities into projects or sprints • Iterate, learn and adapt
Formats	Off-sites 1 or 2 days	Off-sites 1 or more days	• Power Teams (virtual teams) • Pitch Days • Specific business unit deep dives • Employee days • Stakeholder roadshows
Typical audience size	5-15	20-150	Any size
Time to completion	2-3 months	2-3 months	Minimum 3 months

A. ALIGN your North Star and general direction.

The first step is to align. To align means to place or arrange (things) in a straight line, to bring to agreement. In this case it is aligning the North Star and general direction of the company or organisation, so you can get from where you are to where you want to be. We've covered this in chapters 1 to 4.

Once the North Star is set and the first version of the strategy has been created (stage 1), typically by a smaller team like the leadership team, the output then needs to be validated, tested and refined with a wider audience (stage 2). Eventually it will also need to be spread throughout the entire organisation, so it becomes embedded in the way you operate (stage 3). The question is how.

In the next section we will elaborate on how you can address AMPLIFY and ACT.

A good practice we have seen is to constitute a small dedicated team to drive things forward and animate the process. Especially for the work needed to amplify and act.

B. AMPLIFY your North Star and start making waves.

We all know amplification in the context of increasing the volume of sound. Readers familiar with physics might think also of increasing the amplitude of an electrical signal or oscillation. We also refer to the action of making something more marked or intense. Interestingly in genetics, amplification means making multiple copies of a gene or DNA sequence. That is what we are looking for in stage 2. To make the signal stronger, to make more and stronger waves, to make more copies.

Remember where you are: you've had your first session with your senior leadership team as part of stage 1, where you worked on your North Star, your current state, and drafted a first iteration of the Bridge, looking from different angles such as personal and business transformation. Now, it is time to plan stage 2 and amplify the effect of stage 1 so you create more impact.

What works very well after a strategy leadership off-site is to plan a meet-up with an extended group of key stakeholders, often internal, and influencers to explain the why and the what, and allow people to buy into the plan, by challenging it, augmenting it, commenting on it. You allow them to make it better and let them work out how they will put it into action.

This can be done in a fun and co-creative way, in what we typically call an extended leadership conference or off-site. By extended we mean, you can invite a broader group of company leaders including a level down from the group that created the strategy, but also key stakeholders, upcoming talent, and anyone you deem relevant to making the plan better. This could be a group of 50 to 100 people. For such large groups, a good practice is to alternate inspiration with co-creation by putting them to work around specific topics.

The objectives of this type of conference with the extended leadership in stage 2, typically looks like this:

Amplify

1. Open the mind outside-in/inside-out.

2. Gain buy-in on the North Star, strategy and culture.

3. Co-create the Bridge from current to future state (with concrete actions and initiatives).

4. Balance Transforming (innovation excellence) with Performing (operational excellence).

5. Connect as a team, inspire and have fun.

In order to achieve all the above, you'll need to put together a series of activities to draft an agenda.

We'll go through some practices that help achieve the objectives we listed before.

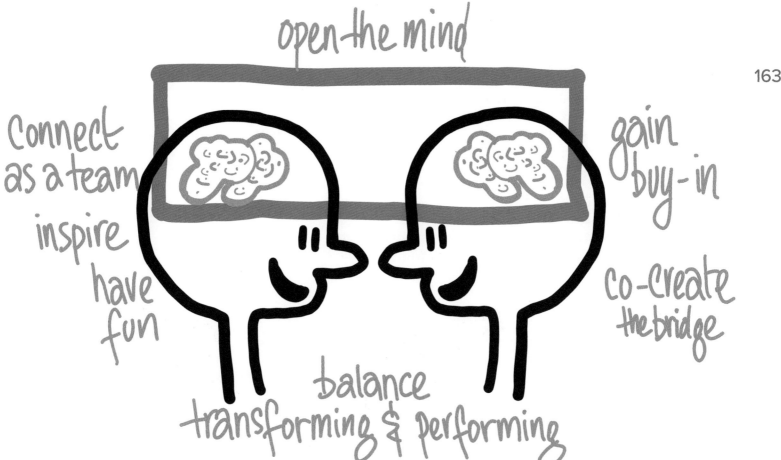

1. OPEN THE MIND

outside-in and inside-out

To open the mind, make sure to include people who can bring in a fresh view. Invite a client, a keynote speaker, a supplier, upcoming talent or a new hire to share something with the wider group. Give them the stage. Let them do their thing, but give them the context and share the objectives of your conference. Why you are organising the event. Why you invited them to speak. At the right we'll list a variety of techniques to involve them. If they are up for it, let them participate in the co-creation sessions. All this can inspire people and stretch the audience to think outside the box.

Outside-in

☑ **Keynotes on trends, transformation, culture or leadership.**

☑ **Testimonial on personal transformation.** We've seen inspiring speakers from outside the organisation, often not even closely related to the industry of the client, that talked about powerful personal transformation.

☑ **Testimonials on business transformation.** Speakers from similar industries, suppliers, partners, or recently acquired companies that share stories about how they addressed business transformation can be very inspiring. Make sure to foresee enough time for Q&A.

☑ **Client presentations** focused on their challenges and opportunities and how they deal with these. If they add where they expect help that can be hugely insightful.

Inside-out

☑ **New hires' view on your company or organisation.** Invite a few new hires to share how they see your company and its culture. How they experienced their first months and how it compares to previous organisations they worked at.

☑ **Key talent vision of the future.** Select a few young, talented employees and give them the stage to present their future vision of your company or organisation. Let them be creative. Give them freedom.

☑ **Lessons learned from success stories and failures.** Create a safe space to have an open conversation and share what you did to succeed or what you learned from a failed project.

☑ **A session on the current state** asking the audience to share what they see: trends, blockers and enablers they see from the internal perspective. Depending on the size of the group you could use sticky notes, knowledge wall, table discussions, flipcharts, etc. but even better is to use digital collaboration tool

2. GAIN BUY-IN ON THE NORTH STAR

including purpose, ambitions, value and culture

Share what's been done before at the leadership summit in stage 1. Keep it light, though. Don't kill your audience with PowerPoints full of words and tables. Just use visuals and keywords covering the four parts of the North Star: Purpose, Ambitions, Value and Culture. Tell a story, invite them to comment.

If you've followed stage 1 as described in Chapters 1 to 4, you should have quite good content and visuals to share. It should be a clear narrative, starting from the current to the future, covering the why, the what and a first stab at the how (Bridge). Explain to the group what came out of the first sessions, highlighting the most important conversations.

The concept of the North Star as we explained in Chapter 2 covers Purpose, Ambitions, Value and Culture.

Explain each of those elements using visuals and why you came up with those. Facilitate a conversation with the audience to reflect, discuss, even challenge. Allow them to digest it and then make it their own.

Culture is critical in this, but very often overlooked or treated separately. We recommend you do this together and make it an integral part of the North Star. What does your current culture look like? What is missing? In Chapter 9 we deep dive on how to drive your culture transformation.

On the right you'll find an example of a fishbowl conversation we ran with hunderd leaders around what a future-proof culture looks like and what it means for a leader. For techniques on how to do this, browse through Chapter 9 which includes various tools.

In the next section we'll also explain how you gain buy-in through co-creation of the bridge towards your future state. You will co-create the details of the bridge to amplify the effects and reach.

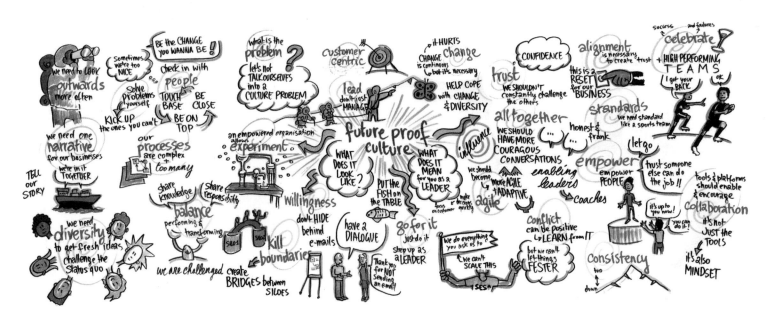

Example of a Fishbowl conversation during a 3-day global SES conference
in Berlin for their top 100 global leaders

3. CO-CREATE THE BRIDGE FROM CURRENT TO FUTURE STATE

with concrete actions and initiatives

Once you've set the scene and explained why you need to transform as an organisation it is time to continue working on the bridge from where you are to where you want to be.

This is similar to co-creating the Bridge in Chapter 4 expect that in this phase you are doing it with a much larger group and need to organise breakouts and appoint team leads for each breakout to facilitate the co-creation.

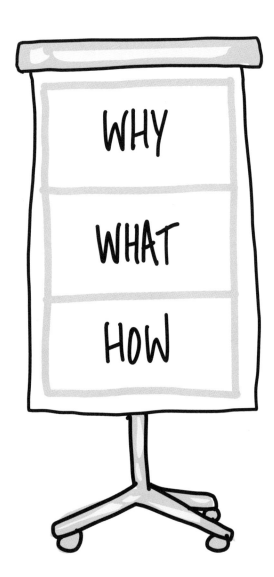

STEPS

Step 1: Select your strategic themes

☑ From the list of ambitions or themes you created earlier (see Chapter 4), pick five to six big strategic themes you want your team to work on.

☑ Assign and brief team leads to run breakout workshops. Keep the process simple.

☑ Break the group up into smaller teams and send them to their breakout rooms.

Step 2: Breakout using the why-what-how questions

☑ Team leads run why-what-how type workshops for each of these selected themes.

☑ Take a flipchart per theme and list the initiatives needed to realise the ambition related for this theme?

☑ Stand up in front of the flipchart and reflect as a team on the why/what/how of each theme. Summarise on one chart.

After you've repeated this for each theme (if not everyone can cover each theme, make sure every team covers at least two or three), you can gather everyone back in the main room.

Step 3: Report back to the group and consolidate

☑ Teams pitch key insights of their session, using the filled-out template flip chart.

☑ Limit time for each team to two to four minutes.

☑ For larger groups you might want to make a selection of the teams that will pitch.

Make sure to have a good description of an initiative, containing an action verb and a result. "Innovation centre" is not a good description. "Build a customer innovation centre" is. You can add due dates and owners later. Keep the flip charts from the breakouts for more detail.

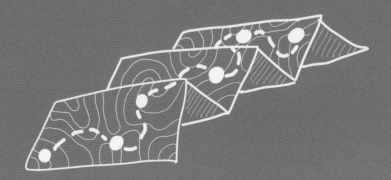

SNAPPY AND FUN DEBRIEFS

Reporting back can be very boring and time-consuming, especially for larger groups. Here are a few tips to make it fun but effective.

TIME-BOXED

How to make it fun but effective...

- Four minutes per report-out.
- Use a timer.
- Play a fun tune when time is up.

What it does to the audience...

- Keep report-outs short and snappy.
- Keeps people's attention.
- Creates a fun atmosphere when people are running out of time.

FORMAT

How to make it fun but effective...

- Use the flip chart template.
- Report the highlights of what you discussed (why/what/how).

What it does to the audience...

- One format makes it easier for the audience to follow, especially when it's time-bound.
- Makes it less boring.

NO REPETITION

How to make it fun but effective...

- Presenter cannot repeat what the others have said.

- Presenter has to keep it short.

- Cover only what's relevant.

What it does to the audience...

- Forces people to listen to other team's report-outs.

- Forces them to make choices on the spot.

- Teaches them to prioritise and tell the story from the flip chart.

4. FIND BALANCE BETWEEN TRANSFORMING & PERFORMING

In these breakouts teams will need to find balance between Transforming (innovation excellence) and Performing (operational excellence). Make sure the output is not all Performing. After all you're meeting to facilitate change, so the focus should be on Transforming, while keeping on Performing.

If your themes are different from the ambitions, they should at least cover the most important problems addressed in your Power Question, your ambitions and the value you intend to create. But also they should have elements that address the purpose and the culture, which drive change in behaviour and can have tremendous impact on the interaction with your stakeholders.

5. CONNECT, INSPIRE & HAVE SOME FUN

Co-creation can be led, but not forced. It requires time, but also foresee time for connecting as a team and having fun. Have enough breaks. Some people might have never met face-to-face so they need time to bond.

All this requires intense planning and live facilitation and moderation. If you have an event-organising capability in-house, use them. If you don't, hire professional (visual) facilitators to help you. A good mix of professional facilitators and occasional event staff can work very well. Getting this right will have tremendous impact on the participant experience and ultimately produces better outcomes.

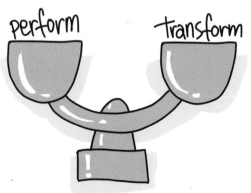

TOOL
CONNECT AND ENGAGE

WARM UPS

The guardian and the footprint

Each person gets two minutes to answer the two following questions. Of which am I the guardian today? What footprint do I want to leave in three to five years from now?

Postcard table

Set up a table with old postcards and ask to pick one and share something personal related to the postcard.

today I am the *guardian* of...

the *footprint* I want to leave behind is...

INTERACTION WALLS

Interaction wall

Each person gets two minutes to answer the two following questions. Of which am I the guardian today? What footprint do I want to leave in three to five years from now?

Elephant wall

Write the big elephants in the room on a Post-it and stick them on a designated elephant wall. You could even ask people to remove their elephants when the issue is resolved. At the end of an off-site look what is left and decide where action is needed.

TOOL
CONNECT AND ENGAGE

INTERACTION EXERCISES

Quizzes

Use mini-quizzes with collaboration tools (like Mentimeter or Slido) to keep them engaged and focused on personal and business related topics. Don't make it all about business.

Fishbowl

Run fishbowl conversations to create a safe environment even in a larger group (see Chapter 9).

Breakout sessions

Organise breakout sessions per table or in separate rooms if the venue offers that facility. Breakouts offer them an opportunity to create a safe environment to speak openly and build action plans together.

GET THEM ON THEIR FEET

Empathy walks

Send them on a walk in pairs. Let them have conversations. Change the pairs for longer walks.

Walk the walls

Invite them to walk around the room and take in the visual harvest that has been created on the wall during the conference.

Personal commitment sheet

Next to the large murals, create personal handouts where they can keep track of their learning and write down personal commitments.

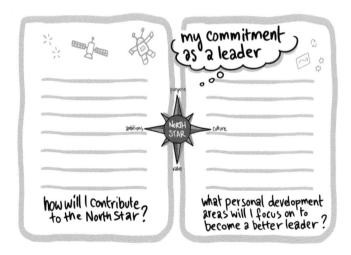

C. ACT to get things done

During stage 2 you have amplified stage 1 with your next level in the organisation such as extended management team and key talent.

You now want to repeat, scale and multiply it to get the transformation going and make it land in different parts of the organisation.

Act

As a follow-up of stage 2, you have some options. We offer a few suggestions. Feel free to adjust or combine elements.

1. Power teams

2. Pitch days

3. Business unit deep dives

4. Employee days

5. Stakeholder roadshows

1. POWER TEAMS

Get organised in Power Teams. These are virtual teams consisting of members of different units that will each work out in more detail what came out of the previous stages, the chosen transformation themes and refine the initiatives and actions that must be taken. At one point they collate it back to the leadership team. Each Power Team will be responsible for one transformation theme.

You can start this during stage 2 by letting them sign up for the theme or ambition they want to work on. It's good practice to have one senior management team member on each theme, but make sure they act as a sponsor, not the team lead. Assign a separate team lead or let the team pick one. After stage 2, let them self-organise.

2. PITCH DAYS

A pitch day traditionally is a sales pitch or promotion made by a company's management team to raise interest from potential investors in an upcoming offer (like an IPO). Potential investors are introduced to the company, its history, and its key personnel. Similarly in the world of start-ups, pitches are an opportunity to introduce a business idea in a

limited amount of time to gain new customers, investors or stakeholders to support your business. TV shows like the Dragon's Den are a good example, allowing upcoming entrepreneurs to pitch their business ideas to a panel of five investors, aka the "Dragons" and ask for financial investment in return for a stake of their company.

Similarly, organising Pitch Days around the transformation themes is a good exercise for the Power Teams to evolve their projects and focus on pitching and storytelling skills, priorities and asks. You brainstorm within a Power Team on a transformation initiative and prepare a 15-minute pitch, explaining the context, the problem, the solution, the value and what you ask from the "dragons".

Pitch days are just one example to follow up and bring a wider audience on board.

3. BUSINESS UNIT DEEP DIVES

Business unit deep dives are similar to the above but run within a specific business unit. It offers the employees of that business unit the chance to reflect on the transformation plans of the overall company or organisation and make it their own.

Typically the business unit manager explains the focus and context, for instance the transformation, and puts participants at work around specific topics. There may be external or internal speakers on relevant topics. It's an opportunity to meet in a different context and share and learn. You could co-create around elements of the North Star, like ambitions, value or culture and deep dive what it means to the business unit and what they will do differently. Create breakouts, use flip charts, report back. All this maximises the sharing and learning.

4. EMPLOYEE DAYS

Many companies use town hall meetings to update employees on company news, financial results, strategy, changes in the organisation and so forth. Those meetings are excellent for updating employees on upcoming transformation plans, but their setting is often not interactive enough to allow employees to work on what the implications are for them. For that we recommend employee days.

Agenda of an employee day

☑ Update on the North Star, ambitions and key values (plenary)

☑ Group conversation: what does that mean for you as individuals (four breakouts)

☑ Workshops on one of the topics (people choose breakout session when they enrol)

☑ Debrief and closing

☑ Dinner and Dance party

5. STAKEHOLDER ROADSHOWS

Stakeholder roadshows are similar to business unit deep dives, but repeatable. Design once, use many times. This is particularly handy when you want to engage internal or external stakeholders, when you can't bring everyone together in one location, or when you have multiple regions to cover. For this type of event, you create an agenda with an update on the North Star, include inspirational injections, and foresee time to put the audience to work on a series of topics. As with business unit deep dives, you capture the results and discussions on flip charts (or get a visual harvester to do so) to keep people engaged. You can then run these roadshows in different locations.

What you have learned...

There are a variety of practices to engage and motivate people across the organisation to get things done. The key is to update them on the big picture and let them work out what this means to them, how they can be part of it and what has to happen to make it successful.

Phase your transformation in three stages: align, amplify and act.

☑ **Align:** starting from what you've done in the first four chapters, you will harvest the essence of stage 1 align to build the next two stages.

☑ **Amplify:** to gain momentum with the wider organisation and increase impact by adding the necessary detail to your strategy and plans, involving the broader organisation, multiplying the effects across your organisation to make sure you get things done across the wider ecosystem.

☑ **Act:** you have a myriad of options to organise follow-up and actions with an extended team, by means of deep dive sessions, pitch days, employee days, roadshows, and many more.

CHAPTER 6
THE POWER OF 3
INSPIRE, VISUALISE AND CO-CREATE

How do you get everyone to act in days, not months?

What you will learn in this chapter...

We'll show you how combining inspiration, visualisation and co-creation will get you more out of your workshops and meetings and will get everyone on board in days, not months. You will learn how to use these three practices from start to finish. These techniques are specifically important for Chapter 5 but they can be applied to the entire journey.

You'll dive deeper into each of these instruments, showing how powerful they can be as individual instruments, before, during and after your meetings and workshops, but you will also feel the power of all three when combining them. It helps with alignment, seeing and sensing from the inside-out and from the outside-in, and motivates everyone to take action. You'll learn how to use it in all phases of your transformation, and with wider communities, even outside of your own organisation.

The Power of 3 will accelerate the process: it will spark imagination, maximise group genius and create a lasting impact.

how do you maximise group genius?
the power of 3
visualise
inspire
co-create
spark imagination
interact
lasting impact
stretch

CHAPTER IN BRIEF

THE POWER QUESTION

How do you get everyone on to act in days, not months?

THE PROBLEM

Often plans addressing complex problems are written by few people. The broader organisation doesn't buy into the plans or are not listened to. The collective intelligence is lost and it takes a lot of time to get everyone on board. This all takes too much time.

THE SOLUTION

Effectively combining inspiration, visualisation and co-creation are an ideal setting to let group genius emerge and to accelerate the process. That allows you to harvest actionable insights sprouting from the collective intelligence and makes your plan succeed.

THE REWARD

The power of these three combined will accelerate the overall process, spark imagination, maximise group genius and create lasting impact.

6.1 HOW DO YOU MAXIMISE GROUP INTELLIGENCE?

We all know how hard it is to build a winning strategy. Many books and articles have been written on this topic. But we also know how hard it is to execute the plan. And even harder to motivate people to take action that were maybe not involved in building the original plan. How do you get everyone on board in days, instead of months? And what if you found a way to harvest the collective intelligence? What if you were able to let group genius emerge?

If you've followed the approach explained in the previous chapters, you will have learned to build your strategy in phases, mapping what your *current reality* is versus the *future* you want to build. And you will have segmented all your input in three levels: *why, what and how.*

The initial sessions usually focus more on the why and the what, and may be light on the how. As you involve more people, you will start adding more detail, especially on the how, adding actions and initiatives to build a more concrete plan.

In all phases of your journey, you will want to make sure everyone is focused on the real problems and gets inspired by the big picture, the why and the what, and gets actively involved in the development and execution, the how. But in all transformations, you will run into people that are reluctant to change or that might even disengage. This can be infectious. You need to avoid losing the big lot. It makes you lose time. Miss momentum. It may even cause your entire plan to fail. At the same time, you want to harvest the best ideas and give attention to the people who are participating. The question now becomes how do you get everyone on board and how to engage the right resource to help you solve your problem.

And when you finally have the right people in the room, how do you harvest the collective intelligence? Some of the greatest scientists have sparked off genius ideas from unexpected encounters with people, animals and nature. Creating the conditions for this to happen pays off. That's why many companies have innovation hubs or incubators where the conditions for group genius can emerge.

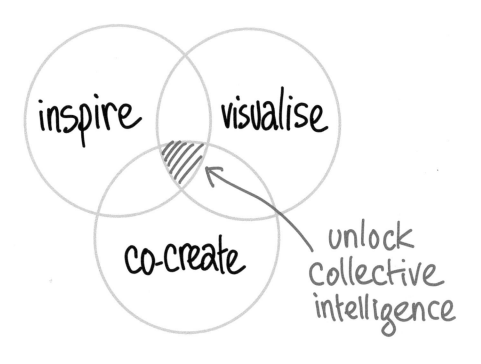

Three ingredients combined can do the trick. These three ingredients are: inspiration, visualisation and co-creation.

Let's unpack each of these and explain what we mean by them. After that we'll also show how you can combine the Power of 3.

A. Inspiration

Taking a step back and looking at where you are and getting inspired by what others have done and where it brought them can create important inflection points, that can cause significant change in your business or industry, turning things in a different direction. Coming up with these type of breakthrough ideas and insights can be stimulated.

You need to inspire people and spark them into getting creative at the start of your transformation journey. Feeling inspired unlocks creativity, enhances productivity, and boosts happiness. People who are inspired are more engaged, are open to learning new things and bringing ideas to fruition, and are far more motivated to take action. Over the past decade, scientists have tested and found strong support that inspiration is a key motivator of creativity.[20]

Inspiration can come from people, but also from the environment they are in. Having tables or not, combining plenary sessions with breakouts in smaller rooms, facilitating conversations, allowing people to write on boards or charts, moving people physically around the room, we've seen how the environment increases participation and impacts on the success of your transformation events, whether they be kick-off, work sessions, or hackathons.

Choose the speakers and topics wisely, making sure they tell stories that:

☑ Inspire

☑ Stretch the audience

☑ Help see new things or from a different perspective

☑ Are short but memorable

☑ Invite them to interact

"Humans think in stories, and we try to make sense of the world by telling stories"
— Yuval Noah Harari

We've also experienced how providing short inspirational injections on specific topics before going into workshops or breakout sessions informs the output of the workshops and creates a better experience throughout the journey.

You can run this in a variety of ways as you saw in Chapter 5. Have an expert or keynote speaker address the topic. Ask one of your team members to take the stage and share insights. Or organise a panel conversation or an interactive session, where a facilitator familiar with the topic facilitates a group of experts, allowing people to comment, share and learn together. These sessions can be eye openers and plant seeds that spark change.

You can easily find interesting examples in your own network or book one or more professional speakers on the various speaking platforms. Pick the ones that you see fit your journey and brief them, so they have context and understand why you invited them to speak.

One of our clients said that these interventions can be great but speakers must be briefed on the context and desired outcome of their intervention to avoid car crashes. He spoke from experience.

B. Visualisation

Inspiring is one thing. Keeping track of the key insights and facilitating action from that inspiration is something else. That's where visualisation comes in.

Visualisation is a technique for creating images, diagrams, or animations to communicate a message. Visualisation helps you prepare how to respond to a situation before it happens. It also helps you achieve your goals by conditioning your brain to see and sense the success in your mind. This is critical for the success of your transformation programme and can accelerate the road to success but also the impact of your plans and actions.

We recommend visually recording or facilitating your meetings and conferences on large murals, in person or virtually. This is called *graphic facilitation*[21] or *visual facilitation*. It stimulates group learning, increases participation and creates a collective memory of the event. It grew out of a network of consultants in the 1970s in the Bay Area in California who were inspired by the approach of designers and architects while problem-solving and collaborating on projects.

Visual refers to the eye, to seeing. Facilitation is making things easy. Visual facilitation consequently is making things easy by using images or graphics. We find examples of messages made easy through graphics everywhere in our daily lives. Think of classrooms, meetings, advertisement, infographics, cartoons, children's books, etc. But also in history visuals and graphics have been instrumental in telling stories, from cave paintings to graffiti, consisting of shapes and images created in an attempt to understand and express the world.

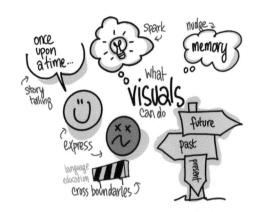

193

The visuals you create during your interactions provide line of sight and clarity on the problems that need solving. Doing it live, in person or virtually, in small or big rooms, helps participants gain insights and accelerates the transformation.

Visualisation, being such a powerful tool, should be far more present throughout the organisation, starting with the leadership and even the board of directors. So, we recommend you try it and start mapping your conversations in words and images. Map your strategic discussions.

Make people see things, not just read things. Draw things out. Use pictures. Working visually makes it easier to see things. It keeps people on board. And it helps them navigate through the content.

There are lots of books and training programmes to get better at visual harvesting. Just go online and find a professional near you that can teach you the basics. For meetings where you want more impact, hire a

Visuals nudge your memory or spark imagination.

Visuals express thought and emotion.

Visuals cross boundaries of language and education.

Visuals can take you back or forward in time.

Visuals tell stories.

professional. Today there is a growing field of professional visual practitioners worldwide that can help you with visual facilitation.[22]

C. Co-creation

Inspiring and visualising does not necessarily move people to act. You need people to feel part of the plan, make it their plan too. You need to facilitate the conversation, so it's a dialogue.

That's where you need co-creation. Co-creation[23] is a process in which input from a broad group of stakeholders is solicited, which, since the 2000s has become a mainstream term encompassing concepts such as participatory and cooperative design and collaborative inquiry (originated in the 1960s–70s). In these processes stakeholders are engaged as co-designers which often helped obtain better results and adoption. After Don Norman, the director of The Design Lab at University of California, coined the term user-centred design in his influential book, Design of Everyday Things, user-centred design evolved towards human-centred design and design thinking more broadly.

"Studies performed on the outcomes of co-creation found participants in co-creative processes experienced increases in individual competence, support for the outcome, perceived legitimacy of process, and strengthened social networks."[24]

While some define it strictly as co-design between organisations and consumers, co-creation is more and more applied to the context of organisational design and ecosystems thinking, including the collaborative design of vision, strategy, process and culture.

Co-creation is now commonly understood as a form of collaborative innovation. Players from various parties (often in and outside the organisation) share ideas and develop solutions together, rather than keeping it to themselves. As such it it seeks to tap into the collective knowledge, creativity, and expertise of all participants to create something that is greater than the sum of its parts.

An essential, sometimes overlooked element of co-creation is the notion of value. Co-creation is just a talking shop if there is no value creation. The value can be personal or business related. Be clear on what happens with the output that is co-created. Will there be follow-up groups, workstreams or teams formed after the co-creation? You could let them self-organise but facilitate the process for instance by allowing them to put their name behind an initiative so they form teams for the next steps.

We've also seen some examples of co-creative organisations that were very agile and self-organised but lacked a common goal and missed a focus on value creation. That ironically leads to more silos. Islands of people co-creating heavily but missing a bigger purpose. This creates unnecessary workarounds, solves the wrong problems, adds waste to the organisation and ultimately doesn't contribute any substantial value to the system they are part of.

Therefore, framing and facilitating co-creation is critical. Putting a group of people to work with tools, flip charts, round table or fishbowl conversations,[25] etc. is great, but give them a topic, a goal, something to work with and document the learning. Start with a Power Question to facilitate the conversation and pick a method that is fit-for-purpose.

Some co-creation examples:

- Why-What-How on a specific problem that has to be addressed in your team.

- A fishbowl on what the ideal culture looks like for your organisation.

- An open round table discussion between various parties and experts on a specific topic e.g. an industry trend.

- Workshops with citizens to gather ideas on a new project in their neighbourhood.

- Organise an elephants-on-the wall exercise, allowing people to stick their elephants on the wall.

When you combine all three, magic happens:

- You'll spark the audience with insights and ideas which will accelerate the transformation process significantly.

- Visualising goals, discussions and insights will help the teams to see what is being discussed and facilitates the business and personal transformation.

- Inspiring keynotes will influence the thinking of attendees and often have immediate impact on how they go back to work or how they work together in a co-creation exercise right after the keynote.

- When you break teams into smaller groups to co-create right after one of more inspiring keynotes and ask the group to visualise key points on a flip chart and use that to report back to the wider group, you're harvesting the collective intelligence.

- Experimenting with facilitation methods that create the right conditions will make people feel safe and speak up more openly.

Microsoft keynote on culture

Country best practices of mental wellbeing

6.2 GET EVERYONE TO ACT IN DAYS, NOT MONTHS

When you organise an event with lots of people, like a seminar or conference, combining inspiration, visualisation and co-creation offers a unique opportunity to tap into the collective intelligence of the people attending. Visuals make it fun and engaging, but also help them to digest the content that is being shared. Inspiration helps create insights, challenges the status quo and stretches them out of their comfort zone. And co-creation is where they see they are not alone, where you tap into the collective intelligence or group genius, where you create the coalition of the willing, a small group of people that lead the change.

These three combined will create the conditions for group genius to emerge. The Power of 3 will maximise and harvest the collective intelligence which will generate co-creative and productive output in a couple of days: something that would otherwise take you months, if you ever even attained what you wanted.

In Silicon Valley and London Hewlett-Packard (and later Hewlett-Packard Enterprise) had co-creation rooms in their Customer Innovation Centres, that were entirely white-boarded. They had an in-house transformation practice of visual facilitators,[26] facilitators and analysts who thoroughly prepared and visually facilitated strategy summits in these rooms aiming to maximise the potential of the invitees. In these facilities they brought together experts with C-suite decision makers and subject matter experts of large corporations and government administrations to work out digital solutions for a variety of problems that were impacting many lives. Also Amazon Web Services (AWS), Price Waterhouse Cooper (PwC), Capgemini and Ernst & Young (EY) have similar practices using visualisation, co-creation and inspiration to accelerate solution development for what is often referred to as "wicked problems".

Things like how to create a cashless society or how to help aspiring farmers in developing countries survive in a sustainable way. If you don't have such capabilities in-house, consider hiring a professional facilitator and/or a visual facilitator to co-design your event. A lot of practitioners have been trained in these powerhouses and are a safe pair of hands for your co-creation challenges.

What you have learned...

You've learned how combining visualisation, inspiration and co-creation can help create the ideal conditions for group genius to emerge and accelerate the outcomes.

☑ **Inspiration** shows you how things can be done differently.

☑ **Visualisation** helps see and harvest insights and takeaways.

☑ **Co-creation** boosts collective intelligence, sharing and group learning.

The Power of 3 will accelerate the process, spark imagination and create more lasting impact.

PART III TRANSFORM YOURSELF & YOUR ORGANISATION

CHAPTER 7

PERSONAL TRANSFORMATION
THE ANATOMY OF A TRANSFORMER

How do you transform
yourself first?

What you will learn in this chapter...

Transforming to secure future business success isn't just about reimagining your company or your strategy, but also reimagining yourself. Have you considered your own personal transformation?

We tend to focus on the analytical part, the mechanics. The human element is often overlooked.

CHAPTER IN BRIEF

THE POWER QUESTION

How do you transform
yourself first?

THE PROBLEM

If you want to transform others,
you need to transform yourself
first. Too many organisations lose
sight of this.

THE SOLUTION

Transforming to secure future
business success isn't just about
reimagining your company or
your strategy, but also
reimagining yourself.

THE REWARD

Personal transformation is how to
move from where you are now to
where you want and need to be.

7.1 PERSONAL AND BUSINESS TRANSFORMATION GO HAND IN HAND

If you want to lead others, you need to start by leading yourself. If you want to transform others, you need to transform yourself first. Too many people in organisations lose sight of this.

Personal and business transformation go hand in hand. They deserve equal attention.

Personal transformation, just like business transformation, is about finding out how you move from where you are now to where you want to be, but also where you need to be. It is about what you say, how you do things and how you behave.

7.2 TOUCH MY HEART BEFORE YOU REACH MY HEAD

Before addressing the transformer in you let us focus on what we know about the brain. It is by far the most complex organ in the human body.[27] It controls thought, memory, movement, feeling, breathing, vision, hearing, smell, all processes that regulate our body. It helps us to sense and experience the world around us. And it merely weighs 1.4 kilograms on average, less than two per cent of your body weight. If you have a heavier brain, rest assured, in most of the cases there is no proven correlation between the weight of your brain and your level of intelligence.

Despite the emerging discipline of neuroscience since the late 20th century, we are still in the very early stages of brain discovery trying to unfold its mysteries. But what do we know?

First, what we do know is that we feel things first so if you want to inspire and transform people, you'll need to touch their heart before your reach their head.

Second, we know the brain has 86 billion neurons and only ten per cent is used. This is a myth, as it's not that we use ten per cent, we merely understand ten per cent. We still don't know how much of our brain is actually being used.

Third, the human body has seven trillion nerves. And you wonder why you have stress? What we know for sure is that some people manage to get on every single one of them. And this is a truth.

As one of our clients commented, we are well informed about practices of the head, to develop analytical skills. That is what we are taught in school, universities and business school. But we lack practices of the heart, focusing on soft skills. The term "soft skills" was created by the U.S. Army in the late 1960s and originally referred to any skill that does not employ the use of machinery. Later on, soft skills became the overarching term for personal attributes that enable someone to interact effectively.

In what follows we'll describe some personal transformation principles and practices that touch the heart.

7.3 THE ANATOMY OF A TRANSFORMER

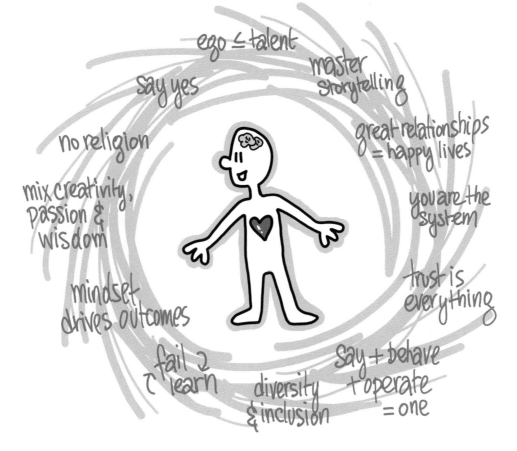

Let us now zoom in on the personal transformation principles. These are the principles that shape the anatomy of a transformer. As a transformer you can deal with anything. You make sense out of what's happening around you and find the energy to respond appropriately.

Principle 1. Your ego shouldn't be bigger than your talent

Too little ego, and you might waste your potential; too much ego and you waste everyone else's. Everybody has an ego. That's why we invented the mirror. But make sure your ego is not bigger than your talent. Too much ego pushes you to a fixed mindset rather than a growth mindset.[28]

Your learning will increase exponentially when you put your ego aside and open your mind to new things.

Checkpoint:

☑ Ask people around you what they think of you. How does it feel? Can you put your ego aside and deal with constructive feedback?

☑ What are you good at? What not? How easy is it for you to acknowledge that?

☑ Have you surrounded yourself with the right talent and learn from working with them?

☑ Learning never stops. Do you want to be a know-it-all, or a learn-it-all?[29]

Principle 2. Say yes more often

When asked to change something, think "Yes, we can" or "Yes, and..." Reactions like "That's not possible", "That won't work", "Yes, but...", "Yes, however..." can't be your standard answer to each new thing crossing your path.

Those that always push back are often energy drainers. They suck the energy away in many conversations, meetings or debates. Imagine someone you know in your private or business life who always starts with "Yes but". You know what we are talking about. This is killing when you want to start something new.

Critical thinkers will come in handy at some point, but you won't get anything done if you start with "no" or "but". Saying yes more often will open doors, will create opportunities.

Checkpoint:

☑ Try saying "yes, we can" or "yes and" more often. How hard is it? What is the impact? What opportunities presented itself after saying yes?

☑ If you come across something that looks impossible, just imagine you already did it and think of the steps that were needed to make it happen. Does it make a difference? What did you learn?

Principle 3. No religion

Do not allow any organisational, technology, product, service or business model religion. Honour your past and define your future. But don't let your legacy stop you from growing. Use it as an anchor, leveraging your capabilities and skills in your new endeavours.

But be willing to question absolutely everything if you truly want to transform. Even if you are the one that created or developed a successful product, service or business model, you will need to be able to let go at certain times to open up for new ways.

Habits, cultures, models or religions are powerful tools that can bring people together and achieve great things, but can also constrain them, tie them down.

Checkpoint:

☑ Look at your rituals and habits. What are your formulas for success? What would happen if you did things radically differently?

☑ Take your biggest success. What capabilities did you need to build it, to deliver it. What did you learn from this?

☑ Could any of these strengths turn into weaknesses if conditions changed?

Principle 4. Mix creativity, passion and wisdom

To innovate, you need to create like a five-year-old. At this age you were extremely creative, not normed by society and free enough to try out everything.

But you also need the passion of a twenty-year-old. Passion will help you create the highest expression of your talent. When you do things with passion, with energy, the people around you feel it.

And finally, you need the wisdom and experience of a sixty-year-old. This will help you evaluate and select the wisest options.

Few people have all these traits, so if you want to innovate, surround yourself with people with different mindsets. It will give you new ideas, new insights, it will make you grow.

215

Checkpoint:

☑ What do you consider your biggest strengths? Check what others say about you. Compare the answers.

☑ Look at the people around you. Are they creative, passionate, wise? What does the mix look like?

☑ What would you need to do to change this? How would you create a better balance?

Principle 5. Mindset drive outcomes

Mindset drives behaviour, behaviour drives culture, culture drives outcomes.

Mindset is attitude. Mindset matters, regardless of age or occupation. Your mindset will determine the outcomes you achieve. Mindset impacts your relationships.

Stanford University psychologist and Professor Carol Dweck, author of Mindset, has described people with a growth mindset as those who believe their abilities can be developed.[30] They believe in persistence in the face of setbacks, seeing failures as essential to mastery, learning from criticism, embracing challenges with agility, and finding lessons and inspiration in the success of others.

Having an open mindset is key to success, so don't shy away from conflict and be open to feedback to keep challenging your own thinking.

Checkpoint:

☑ What is your dominant mindset? Do you like change or does it scare you?

☑ Plot your dominant mindset and behaviours on a sheet of paper. Plot also the main outcomes you achieved.

☑ Now plot your dominant mindset and behaviours from five, ten or more years ago on a sheet of paper. Same for the main outcomes of that period.

☑ Compare both. Is your mindset very different? Do you behave differently today? Is there a difference in the outcomes?

☑ What do you learn from this?

Principle 6. Experiment, fail and learn

Through a lot of experimentation, you may eventually achieve a few successes, but probably you'll fail many more times. What is important is that you draw valuable lessons from your mistakes. This means you should tolerate failures to start with. Analyse where it went wrong and what competences you are missing to succeed.

Build competences in the process or go find people with competences that you lack, so you get coached or can tap into them when you need them.

217

Checkpoint:

☑ Look at your biggest failures. What lessons have you drawn from them?

☑ Are you aware of your incompetences? Do you just accept your incompetences, or do you also take action to build new competences? What measures have you taken to avoid making the same mistakes.

☑ Do you share your failures and learnings with others transparently?

☑ What (else) can you do differently?

Principle 7. Embrace diversity and inclusion

There is no inclusion without diversity. Creating an environment where everyone feels valued and respected is critical for success. Recognising and valuing the unique differences and similarities among individuals, groups and organisations enriches societies, companies and any kind of team. These include differences in race, ethnicity, gender, sexual orientation, age, abilities, religion, culture, and socio-economic status.

Checkpoint:

☑ How do you embrace diversity and inclusion on a daily basis?

☑ How diverse is your environment? How many of your friends or co-workers are of different race, ethnicity, sexual orientation, religion, socio-economic status?

☑ What are the pros and cons of this type of environment? What could you change? What impact would it have?

Principle 8. Success is where say, behave and operate are one

Success can only be achieved if you put your money where your mouth is. Just talking will not change anything. But operating without talking to others might also not be getting you the results you want. In other words, you need to align what you say, how you behave and how you operate to succeed. This includes purpose, culture, processes, structures, budgets, incentives, policies, etc. You have to "walk the talk".

If, on top of this, it's all aligned to what you think, your personal values and purpose, then you are truly equipped for success. This means that you are truly honest with yourself.

219

Checkpoint:

☑ Are your actions and behaviours in line with what you say, with what you believe?

☑ Are you helping people around you when you see they are not aligned?

Principle 9. Trust is everything

Trust is the basis of a cohesive and well-functioning teams. It is essential for performing, but even more so for transforming. When under pressure cohesive teams perform better.

If there is no trust your team might fear debate and avoid conflict, they might not buy in or commit to decisions taken, they will not feel accountable, and they will not deliver the results. Trust provides psychological safety needed to tackle the changes ahead. Trust will stimulate open dialogue and constructive conflict, decision-making and commitment, initiative and accountability which will ultimately deliver results.[31]

Trust is earned. It doesn't come with a title. Trustworthiness is something we feel. Trust is the result. Once it's lost it's very hard to get back.

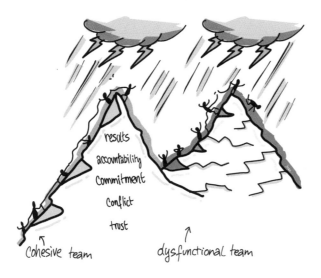

results
accountability
Commitment
Conflict
trust

Cohesive team   dysfunctional team

Checkpoint:

☑ Are you trusting people? Are you trustworthy yourself? How come?

☑ Are you able to resolve conflicts easily?

☑ How do you behave when put under pressure? How does it affect your performance? How does it impact how you behave in your team?

Principle 10. You are the system

Do you sometimes say: "I'm really sorry. It's not me. It's the system" or "We can't do this, because it is not the way we do things around here." System can mean company, government, organisation, team or even society.

Stop saying that. You are the system. There is no such thing as the company myth or the system myth. The sum of all individual parts makes the system. If you want to change the system, start with yourself. You can make small differences every day.

Every individual can start a transformation of their own and form a coalition of the willing to snowball into a larger impact.

This applies to all sorts of systems, including teams, companies, public administrations, NGOs, even countries.

Checkpoint:

☑ Do you catch yourself saying or thinking: "It's not me. It's the system?" What does this tell you?

☑ What options do you have to change that? What have you already done?

☑ What could you do differently to have more impact?

Principle 11. Great relationships build happy lives

In life, relationships are essential for your happiness and success. And so are ecosystems where these relationships develop. In nature, each organism has its function and interacts with a physical environment. The same goes for business or personal ecosystems. Water it. Cultivate it. Give it time. Do not expect immediate return from relationships. That's not how it works.

We were joking when writing this stating: "Do not ask what your relationships can do for you, but what you can do for your relationships." It's funny but it's true. Invest in your relationships and maintain them. One day someone may return a favour that you need or may open the door you needed to open. It might even be that you have never done anything for this person, but for someone else in their network. These small favours will help you a great deal during any transformation.

Checkpoint:

☑ What have you done for your network lately? When was the last time someone called you for a favour? How did you respond?

☑ How easily could you tap into your network to ask for a favour? Would you ask for a favour for someone else? Even if it's just opening a door.

Principle 12. Master storytelling

"Your ability to persuasively sell your ideas is the single greatest skill that will help you achieve your dreams."[32] Storytelling taps into people's imagination, inspires them and creates a connection. Storytelling will help you get people on board in any transformation and inspire them to action. Stories are compelling pitches that help explain what you see, what you think must happen and what you need from others.

When transforming you will need to act like a field journalist reporting on the journey. Updating people on where you are, what worked, what didn't work and what you learned. But just like a field journalist, make sure to get your story straight. The facts should check out. Unfortunately people often remember lies much longer than the truth.

223

Checkpoint:

☑ Are you telling stories or presenting facts? How easily can you convey a message?

☑ Do you use details that appeal to your audience? Do you make it personal? Are your stories relatable?

☑ Are you creating a connection with your audience when you tell your story? Are your stories inspiring?

BEFORE ASKING OTHERS TO TRANSFORM, START BY TRANSFORMING YOURSELF.

7.4 SO, WHAT CAN YOU DO WITH THOSE TWELVE PRINCIPLES?

When you start transforming towards your desired future, try to stay true to yourself. Do it in an authentic way. "Be yourself no matter what they say."[33] Simply put, being authentic is about staying true to who you are, to what you do and to your purpose.

And remember before you ask others to transform, start by transforming yourself.

We suggest the following:

☑ Take time to go through the checkpoints to assess your personal current reality.

☑ Ask feedback from people around you and be open to their input.

☑ See where you may have gaps and decide which ones you want to develop. Build your own bridge.

☑ Identity your strengths and weaknesses.

☑ Get out there and find opportunities to learn. Talk about it to people. Look for mentors or coaches in those areas.

☑ Start your personal transformation. You won't regret it!

What you have learned...

☑ If you want others to transform, you need to **transform yourself first.**

☑ **Personal transformation** is how to move from where you are now to where you want and need to be.

☑ **Twelve principles** with checkpoints that help you to transform yourself.

CHAPTER 8
BUSINESS TRANSFORMATION
MAKE IT A STRATEGIC CAPABILITY

How do you turn transforming
into performing?

What you will learn in this chapter...

While reimagining your future, visions might change, strategies will (dis)appear, cultures will evolve, and organisational structures could be turned upside down to make room for something new.

The question we address in this chapter is how you can turn transformation into a strategic capability to anticipate or respond to big changes, build new solutions and to scale fast when needed? Or how do you turn Transforming into Performing.

let's do this again !!
just hit refresh I am ready
scale fast
resilience
innovation strategies
transformational change
culture of trust

CHAPTER IN BRIEF

THE POWER QUESTION

How do you turn transforming
into performing?

THE PROBLEM

Change is the only constant.
Although many organisations
have innovation capabilities,
they are often focused on
incremental innovation, but lack
the transformational capability to
respond to the constant change,
build new solutions and scale
those quickly.

THE SOLUTION

To become resilient as an
organisation, to perform and to
scale fast, you have to build in
transformation as a
strategic capability.

THE REWARD

You'll overcome disruptions more
easily, anticipate or respond
more quickly to market changes
and you'll be able to transform
successfully whenever needed.
Your transformation will turn
into performing.

8.1 THE WHY, WHAT AND HOW OF BUSINESS TRANSFORMATION

Let us start by defining the why, what and how of business transformation and when it becomes a strategic capability. We've written it down in a sentence. It turned out to be rather long – we apologise in advance:

> **A business transformation is a strategic capability when it offers...**
>
> **what**
> ... the ability to **stay young, hit refresh, future-proof** or **reimagine** your **North Star** (purpose, ambitions, value, culture), **strategy and leadership ready for the fast-paced world**
>
> **HOW**
> ... by **rebalancing existing or adding new investments** (iterate, innovate, disrupt) in **products, services, processes, markets, platforms and business models**
>
> **WHY**
> ... to drive future **profitable growth** and sustainable value in the **customer, employee** and **ecosystem**, while taking care **of the planet**.

If you want to turn transformation into a strategic capability, you will need to be willing to challenge every aspect of your business: your North Star, your business model, your operating model, your people, your culture, even yourself.

You cannot rest on your laurels. You can honour your legacy, which serves present performance, but you must be willing to sacrifice parts of it to help the transformation come true and build a new performing legacy.

The first step in deriving more value from your transformation and innovation investments is to define the outcome you're trying to achieve. As covered in Chapters 1 to 4 you start by finding your North Star and agreeing on your future state, with its four essential components: purpose, ambitions, value and culture. And finally, you build your Bridge, your strategic plan, to move from your current to your desired future.

the ability to stay young & hit refresh, future proof or re-imagine your North Star, strategy & leadership ready for the fast-paced world

Your organisation will need to have the right mix of performing and transforming capabilities. That is a condition to succeed in any major transformation and enables you to have transformation as a strategic capability.

What capabilities do you need to develop for this to come true?

Transformation as a strategic capability

A. Pick the right yin and yang at the top

1. The visionary leader and the operational leader
2. Capability focused leadership
3. Leadership style and diversity

B. Power your innovation strategy

1. The operating model for both running the day-to-day and building your future
2. The traditional R&D and business model innovation muscle
3. Sixteen innovation strategies

C. Value people as the soul of your business

1. A culture of trust
2. The coalition of the willing and the floaters
3. Tension management

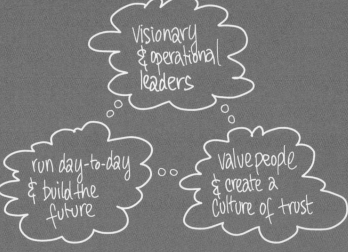

A. Pick the right yin and yang at the top

Equally important is to reimagine your leadership, including your board of directors. No transformation has been successful without it.

1. THE VISIONARY LEADER AND THE OPERATIONAL LEADER

The most successful organisations have the right performing and transforming yin and yang at the top. A strong transformer at the top, a visionary and innovative leader capable of inspiring the troops and navigating the ship, supported by a strong performer, the operational leader behind the buttons in the engine room that can operationalise that vision and keep the ship afloat.

Let us look at some examples:

Apple: Before Jobs died, COO Tim Cook, the performer, and CEO Steve Jobs, the transformer, were the perfect twins. Jobs' visions, ideas and designs had to be executed and Cook was that executional leader. After Jobs passed away Cook took over as CEO and continued Apple's incredible growth. However, Apple has become less disruptively innovative since then as Tim has less of that imaginative and inspirational capability that Jobs had allowing him to see things others didn't. Since Cook took over Apple's innovation has been more focused on continuing the business model and adding new services and features.

Microsoft: Until January 2000, Steve Ballmer and Bill Gates were the yin and yang of Microsoft. Ballmer was the COO and operational leader. Gates was the CEO and visionary. Ballmer succeeded Gates as CEO from 2000 to 2015. Under his tenure Microsoft's growth and expansion carried on. However, in spite of its business performance, Microsoft lost its cool and North Star. Satya Nadella took Ballmer's place and became CEO in 2014. Nadella has those unique skills to be both a transformer and a performer and hit the refresh button soon after his appointment. In 2022 Microsoft was again ranked third place in the list of most valuable companies in terms of market capitalisation. Just after Apple and Saudi Aramco.

futureproof

Tim Cook
Steve Ballmer
Sheryl Sandberg
Elon Musk ??

perform   transform

Steve Jobs
Bill Gates
Marc Zuckerberg
Elon Musk

leadership

Facebook/Meta: At Facebook Sheryl Sandberg, COO, and Mark Zuckerberg, CEO, worked in tandem for more than fourteen years. Sandberg was the performer, Zuckerberg the transformer. After joining Facebook in 2008, Sandberg quickly began to focus on how to make Facebook profitable and convinced the board to start relying on advertising, as opposed to the company's focus of "building a really cool website" prior to her joining. Sandberg was credited for making the company profitable. Sandberg defined the COO role rather broadly heading advertising, sales, marketing and business development, not making it easy for her replacement, Javier Olivan, who became the Chief Growth Officer when she stepped down in October 2022.

Tesla: CEO Elon Musk is a transformer and performer. Seen as a genius by many. He didn't really have a true operational leader in the first years of Tesla and micromanages at the start of each venture. Next to Tesla he also heads SpaceX, SpaceLink and Twitter. Meanwhile he hired multiple operational leaders for his various business ventures. His tendency to be all-around has raised many eyebrows and impacted his credibility.

Those unique transforming and performing twins at the top are a rare find. Most companies will need to go above and beyond headhunting those capabilities at the top. The next best alternative is to balance your leadership and board with a good mix of performers, transformers and those that can do both in your organisation.

2. CAPABILITY FOCUSED LEADERSHIP

In the past years we've seen an explosion of new C-suite titles like Chief Innovation Officer, Chief Sustainability Officer, Chief Data Officer, Chief Customer Officer. On top of having a tandem of transformers and performers at the top, it is key to identify the roles you need to build or strengthen the must-have capabilities to successfully deliver future success and build your North Star. The leadership team mix must reflect those ambitions.

Apple was one of the first in the tech industry to appoint a Chief Design Officer, reflecting Apple's obsession with design. "Design isn't just what it looks like and feels like – design is how it works." Steve Jobs.[34] Microsoft appointed a Commercial Partner Corporate Vice President to focus on building a strong ecosystem, one of their North Star ambitions.

In "The Invincible Company", Strategyzer introduces an interesting concept. That is to hire a Chief Entrepreneur acting as co-CEO with dedicated staff focused on the disruptive innovation in your organisation. This fully empowered co-CEO focuses on the transforming part of the company, and tests new products, business models and corporate venturing initiatives. The traditional CEO focuses on running the company, the performing part. Needless to say both will require strong bridge-builders for this model to work.

"To build an invincible company you need to create, manage and harmonize two completely antagonistic cultures under one roof."[36] – Alexander Osterwalder

Although the co-CEO model is still rather rare today, a 2022 study[35] in the Harvard Business Review found that companies listed with co-CEOs generated an average annual shareholder return of 9.5% – significantly better than the average of 6.9% for each company's relevant index. Nearly 60% of the companies led by co-CEOs outperformed. Examples of organisations that have or had co-CEOs are Barco, Chipotle, Goldman Sachs, Netflix, Oracle, PIMCO, Salesforce, SAP, Workday and Unilever.

3. LEADERSHIP STYLE AND DIVERSITY

What talent should you bring on board at the leadership level to challenge traditional thinking, generate new ideas and execute the transformation you need? This will require specific necessary skills, behaviours, experiences, co-creation and diversity.

We all tend to surround ourselves with people that are like us, with a similar background or active in the ecosystem or industry we already know. That happens also at the top. A leadership team that lacks diversity might think alike and see things the same way. This kind of group thinking can be powerful but also dangerous. To promote diversity in leadership, you must ensure a healthy mix of people that think, feel and act differently. Leaders that challenge each other, that look for new ecosystems, want better customer experiences and embrace new business models. The kind of leaders that can identify and build and scale new capabilities fast.

239

"CEOs and the traditional leadership staff are generally excellent at growing and running a company within a known business model. But they often fall short at the task of innovating future growth engines."[37]

— Alexander Osterwalder

Next to the diverse talent that you need, it is important to reflect on the leadership style. What is your leadership style and what can you learn from other leadership styles to boost innovation and even disruption?

Transformational Practices at Singularity University, explored the four profiles of exponential leadership needed to truly innovate and disrupt in an inspiring article.[38] She identified a series of critical skills leaders must learn to successfully navigate in a rapidly changing world – not just to create strategic advantage for their organisations, but also to help build a more inclusive and equitable future for all. We've read it through and visually harvested the key insights.

technologist

obsessed with (new) tech

adopting early

understanding exponential curves

shifting course

disruptive

building "unholy" partnerships

engineering R&D

crowdsourcing

humanitarian

doing good

catalysing

higher purpose

connecting across industries

sustainable

promoting diversity of ideas & engagement

empowering

unlocking

Ask yourself how your current leadership team would fit with people that think, feel and act differently, not how those people fit with them.

What does this mean for your board of directors?

If you have a board of directors, ultimately you will have to hit refresh at board level as well, challenge their capabilities and the composition of your board to appropriately support the North Star in all its aspects. How can the board help transforming to reach its ambitions? How can they help foster innovation? How can they push the needle on the company's innovation agenda?

When asked in an interview what makes him angry, Ignace Van Doorselaere, CEO of the Belgian Chocolatier Neuhaus, replied: "People on boards of directors that want to make themselves interesting. Figureheads like Statler and Waldorf[39] from the Muppet Show, who think they always know better, but actually have little useful to say. Boards of directors exist to make management better, not to talk about personal glory days or pose slogans".[40]

You need a board that endorses the North Star with inside-out and outside-in insights by enhancing their own innovation literacy, knowledge and learning. They should value diversity, stimulate creative thinking, embrace risk, value disruptive thinking, have frank conversations with room for conflict, and hire/develop the CEO to lead the performing and transforming side of the business.

B. Power your innovation strategy

1. THE OPERATING MODEL FOR RUNNING THE DAY-TO-DAY AND BUILDING YOUR FUTURE

What operating rhythms and organisational processes will help you to get to the new North Star (transform) and respond to the demands of today (perform)?

The disadvantage of large organisations can also be an advantage. The ongoing business provides you funds to fuel your transformation, something start-ups don't have. The people already working for you allow you to scale faster than start-ups. The systems and processes make your delivery more robust and reliable. But your leadership must show the way. They need to be ambassadors of your (new) North Star. Your mechanisms and structures to manage the current reality so you feel more in control need to be balanced with governance structures that help you innovate and disrupt.

"Balance the transforming and performing agenda of your future success and the running of the day-to-day."
– Philips former CEO Frans van Houten – reflects performing and transforming in its scorecard, reviews, targets, objectives.[41]

If you are serious about the transformation, your leadership team should spend at least 30% of their time on the needed innovation to build the future and the remainder 70% on executing the present.

The governance model needs to reflect that and promote both performing and transforming:

- Find the right rhythm of the business to review and develop the performing and the transforming sides of the business.

- Agree on scorecard metrics and targets that will measure the success of the performing (Key Performing Indicators) and transforming (Transformation Leading Indicators) sides of the business.

- For the transforming side enable dynamic reallocation of resources with fast decision-making and HR to support this.

- Enable your ability to nurture your innovation and develop some of the sixteen strategies mentioned below.

The performing and transforming speedometer (scorecard)

OPERATIONAL EXCELLENCE	INNOVATION EXCELLENCE
Performing Short Term	Transforming Long term
Profit, People & Customer of TODAY	Profit, People & Customer of TOMORROW
Iterate and Operate	Innovate and Disrupt
Do and Execute	Think and Create
Productivity, Efficiency and Effectiveness	Activities and Behaviours

When measuring **operational excellence**, you will focus on the doing and the execution of your short-term day-to-day business measured on a daily, weekly, monthly, quarterly or yearly basis. Your focus is to enhance iteratively your productivity, efficiency and effectiveness of what you do. You'll want to have a good mix of operating P&L (e.g. revenue, gross margin, cost acquisition, cost), share (e.g. percentage of addressable market, new markets), customer (e.g. satisfaction, Net promotor Score, virality-impress PR) and people (e.g. happiness index, employee satisfaction, speed of onboarding) metrics. Your focus is the return on investment. Those metrics are your **Key Performance Indicators (KPI)**.

When measuring **innovation excellence**, you will focus on the elements that show you are going in the right direction using the North Star as a compass. Your intention is to think strategically, create new innovations and/ or potentially disrupt. You will also need to make sure behaviours of the organisation have evolved to enable the transformation at hand. You would have metrics related to your innovation practice (e.g. number of ideas generated, experiments, prototypes, interviews, customer validation), management (e.g. number of products in pipeline, in problem/ solution fit, in product-market fit, in products at scale, #validated business models) and strategy (e.g. new type of partners, ecosystem maturity, ventures, start-up partnerships, products and business models scaling). Your focus is the return of learning and investment. We call those metrics **Key Transformation Indicators (KTI)**.

Keeping both in balance requires you to be aligned and efficient in the management of today's business demands but also adaptive to changes around you. Today's leaders have to be like Janus, the Roman God of transitions and dualities, of doorways, gates and transitions, of beginnings and endings. He had two faces looking in opposite directions, one facing the past, and one facing the future.

To build your metrics you can use the results of the exercise in The North Star Chapter 2 where you determine the value you want to deliver for each of your main stakeholders. Be very selective, do not go over thirty KPIs and KTIs in total.

"In our scorecards we measure both performing and transforming. In our reviews we talk about both. And the targets I give to all my executives... always include some transform objectives."[41]

— Frans van Houten, former CEO Philips

2. THE TRADITIONAL R&D AND BUSINESS MODEL INNOVATION MUSCLE

Successful innovation needs innovation in the traditional product, services R&D and technology area, innovation in the Business R&D and great execution.[42]

Having great products and technologies is a first step. But creating the value proposition that customers want and finding the business model to grow revenues profitably will guarantee much better returns. This requires going beyond the traditional technology, service and product innovation to build the muscle on how you can deliver better value to your customers and build new scalable business models. Your business model helps you to create, deliver and capture value.

Despite what many (used to) believe, it's not always the best product or service that wins. It's often underestimated how much effort needs to be put into competing with superior

successful innovation = traditional product, services & technology R&D + business R&D + execution

business models versus innovating on the product, service and technology. But be mindful because you might be dependent on factors out of your control, and you may need a few intermediate business models before getting it right.[43]

As an example, Netflix had for some time considered offering movies online, before launching their streaming offer in 2007. They started as an online DVD rental business in 1998 with the vision to move to streaming. The original idea was a "Netflix box" that could download movies overnight, ready to watch the next day. But it was only in the mid-2000s that data speeds and bandwidth costs had improved sufficiently to allow customers to download movies from the net. After witnessing how popular streaming services like YouTube were, even without high-definition content, they dropped the concept of a digital box and focused on streaming.

How much effort – time, resources, money, people – do I currently put in innovating my business?

Let's simplify innovation and categorise it in three types of innovation, using the machine metaphor:

Iterative innovation
this is oiling the current machine to make it more productive, more efficient or effective. Your focus is to make a better version of what you have today.

Innovative innovation
this is adding a new part to the existing machine. Your focus is to create something new that wasn't there before.

Disruptive innovation
this is about building a new machine. Your focus is to build something radically new that changes the rules of the game, that disrupts someone else or even yourself.

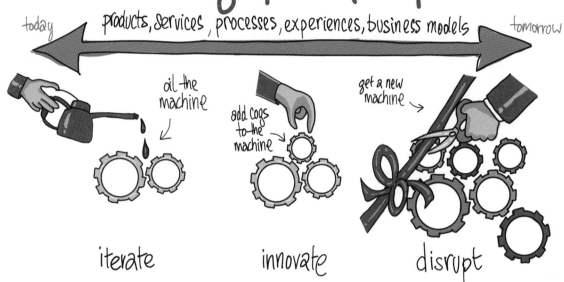

In our experience many organisations spend 90% (commercial) to 95% (public entities) in the iterate bucket and 5 to 10% in the innovate bucket and neglect the disrupt bucket. In contrast, successful transformative organisations spend 70% in the iterate bucket, 20% in the innovate bucket and 10% in the disrupt bucket. High Tech companies even go beyond and spend around 50%, 30% and 20% in each respective bucket.

We recommend you categorise your running and planned projects and resources over those three buckets and see what consumes most resources. You might be surprised about the outcomes. It will mirror how well you are balancing transforming and performing.

A CEO that is not spending 30 to 40% of his time on the innovative part is not really serious about it. The same goes for the entire leadership team.

3. SIXTEEN INNOVATION STRATEGIES

How do you define what innovation strategies you need for your transformation? How can you do this internally? How do you create partnerships, ecosystems and leverage the unlimited talent outside the company? How can we create soulful, highly energised future-proof organisations and individuals ready to transform and innovate?

People and business struggle to determine how to get started or how to make the next steps in their transformation that involves new ways of innovating the business.

We have mapped the strategic options into the following sixteen quadrants.

- On the horizontal axis, you will find the degree of openness from internal to externally focused from low to high.

- On the vertical axis, you will find the level of commitment from low to high.

The eight quadrants on the left are the innovation strategies you execute internally while the eight quadrants on the right cover your externally driven innovation, also referenced as corporate venturing.

You don't need to cover them all but aspire to balance inside with outside focused partnerships to innovate. Leverage your partnerships, ecosystem and the unlimited talent outside the company. What is important is to contextualise it for your business. To select what works for you, start experimenting and scale
for impact.

Which of the sixteen are you doing today?
Which ones will you sustain or accelerate?
What do you need to stop?
Which ones should you start or try out?

corporate venturing

		joint venture	M&A
future proof leadership & culture	R&D + engineering		
intrapreneur & innovation programs	innovation lab	Strategic partnership & ecosystem	corporate venture capital
Communities	internal accelerator & incubator	cocreation community	external incubator & accelerator
training & mentoring	agile governance	advisory board	innovation events HACK this

high ← low : level of innovation Commitment

internal ← → external : degree of openness

C. Value people as the soul of your business

1. A CULTURE OF TRUST

Trust is fundamental when building the right leadership culture. Your leadership needs to breathe and behave according to the why, what and how of your North Star in everything they do. Often underestimated, culture is actually the hardest nut to crack. It is one of the main reasons transformations fail.

A CEO that believes and acts as a sponsor of the transformation must allocate at least 30 to 40% of his or her time to the transformation at hand. If you want to know more about developing a culture aligned to your North Star we'll explain that in detail in Chapter 9 when we talk about Heartset, Mindset and Actionset.

This public display of confidence by the leaders in the North Star will increase the trust in the transformation. And trust is at the heart of high-performing and transforming teams. You'll need to trust your peers but also show that you can be trusted. Setting clear expectations towards each other and agreeing on accountability will be a tremendous help here.

When evaluating people or leaders who didn't meet their goals, Jørgen Vig Knudstorp, CEO of Lego from 2001 to 2016, didn't blame them for failing. He blamed them for failing to ask for help and others for failing to give help.

Trusting each other improves collaboration. And your collaborative strengths will increase your success rate in solving company-wide challenges. It helps you outperform the competition. It enables you to anticipate market changes. It will drive your ambitions.

"When you take good care of your employees, they will take good care of your customers." This a statement that addresses company or organisational culture. It is a fundamental aspect of transformation, but you also need it to perform.

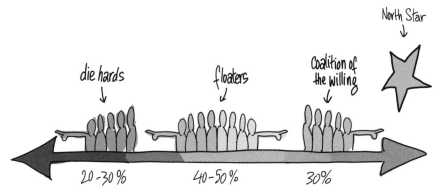

2. THE COALITION OF THE WILLING AND THE FLOATERS

Most people will not resist small, incremental changes. Big transformations are much harder as people need to let go of things and of their comfort zones. People don't resist the change itself, but the pain it causes them and the uncertainty it creates.

When starting a transformation, our experience shows that you typically have 30% of people that are with you in the transformation towards your North Star. In transformation change these are often called the coalition of the willing. The term originally refers to an international alliance focused on achieving a particular objective, of military or political nature. In the context of transformation, they are the most enthused audience willing to undertake the new journey. But there is also usually a group of around 50 % in the middle that are doubting, not sure they understand why or how they should transform. You could call them the floaters, the swing voters, they are undecided. And then you usually have around 20% heavily resisting the change, being negative or sometimes even confused.

The pitfall is to spend far too much time trying to convince those resisting the change, which slows down the transformation programme. This causes them to lose momentum, even confuses the floaters and slows down or even stops the coalition of the willing. Accept that a portion of people will never be convinced and might need to leave the organisation or will leave on their own when they disagree with the new North Star. Spend most of your time and energy fuelling the coalition of the willing and convincing the floaters. And always keep your eyes on the North Star.

3. TENSION MANAGEMENT

When transforming and performing at the same time you will need to manage possible tensions between operational and transformational goals with discipline and strong leadership.[44] Transparent communication is crucial here. Take your time to acknowledge the tensions, empathise with each other and speak up. This will require strong facilitative leadership. Some tension and contrasts can produce results and force people to be creative. Too much tension will kill the transformation so find the right tension.

Many organisations struggle with the tension between transforming and performing. On the one hand, there is value in learning from experimentation and failure. On the other hand, you must manage pressure and well-being and still deliver results. Great leaders openly and transparently acknowledge that tension and protect their people

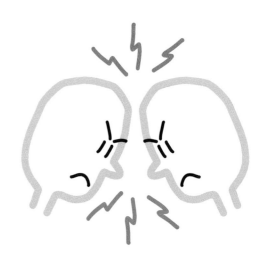

Tension management

Tolerance for failure	No tolerance for incompetence
Value Learnings from failure	Value outstanding performance
Culture of innovation	Continue to seek legacy business growth
Willingness to experiment	Rigorous discipline
Safe to speak	'Brutally' honest
Highly collaborative	High level of individual accountability
Achieve long term goals	Short term goals
Caring for well-being	Drive for results and accountability
Ideal future	Present day-to-day realities

8.2 TOP TWENTY BUSINESS TRANSFORMATIONS OF THE PAST DECADE

When you look at the top twenty business transformations of the past decade published by Harvard Business Review you can observe some clear patterns mentioned above. Companies like Netflix, Development Bank of Singapore (DBS), Microsoft, and Philips had the following in common:

The study approached business transformation success from three different angles:

- Effective repositioning of the core business to changes or disruptions in its markets, giving its legacy business new life

- Creation of new growth by creating new products, services, markets, and business models

- Attainment of robust financials

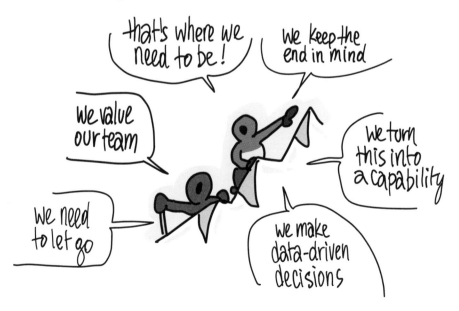

They all demonstrated most of the transformational capabilities that we covered in this chapter:

1. **They were ready to reinvent themselves, building a new North Star.** Not afraid to let go of the legacy and leverage the core capability to reposition its core while entering new growth areas.

2. **They showed the right leadership capabilities to transform** striking the right balance between operational and innovation excellence. They were able to operate quickly in reviewing strategies or relocating resources where needed.

3. **They saw digital as an enabler, providing oxygen to the company.** As such they seized the digital opportunity, making data-driven decisions and leveraging technology for new platforms and novel superior business models.

4. **They put customers at the heart of their company.** They always kept the customer in mind. Instead of thinking about customers, they started thinking like customers.

5. **They valued people as the soul of the company.** They saw culture as the backbone of the organisation with people being part of the transformation. They understood that If you take care of your people, they will take care of your customers.

6. **They turned transformation into a strategic capability.** They were able to reinvent the core business giving its legacy systems a new life and created new growth with new products, services and business models.

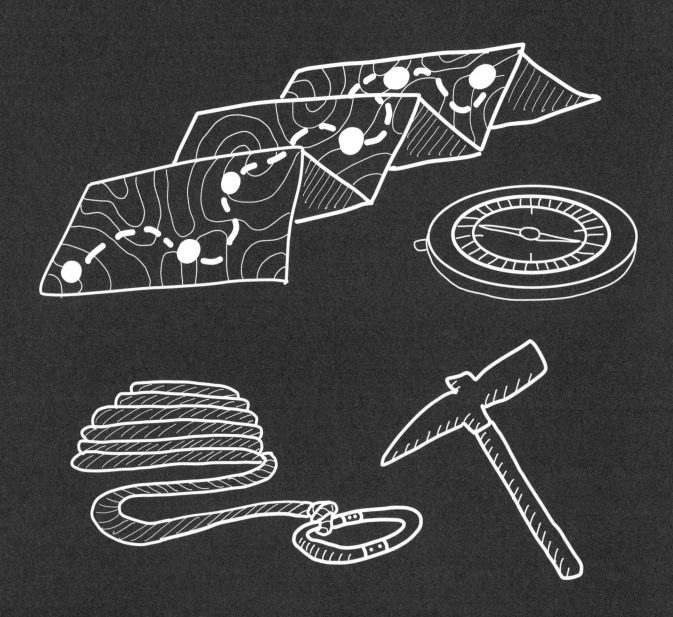

What you have learned...

☑ How you can **turn transformation into a strategic capability** to anticipate or respond to big changes, build new solutions and scale those quickly.

☑ To develop the right capabilities you will need to:

- **Pick the right yin and yan at the top.**

- **Power your innovation strategy.**

- **Value people as the soul of your business.**

☑ If you do so, you will be able to **turn Transforming into Performing**.

CHAPTER 9
CULTURE TRANSFORMATION
HEARTSET, MINDSET AND ACTIONSET

How do you start changing behaviours?

What you will learn in this chapter...

Culture as part of your North Star cannot be underestimated. Reflecting on your desired culture supporting your North Star is therefore fundamental as shown in Chapter 2.

263

Organisational culture evolves over time. It is based on the shared beliefs, values, and norms of an organisation. It creates a unique identity, a sense of purpose and belonging. Those can be implicit or explicit.

For organisations seeking to become more transformative and innovative, culture change is often the most challenging part.

Activating and living your culture needs time to sink in and perseverance. Leaders should role model the behaviours but creating a culture that drives performance requires leadership and its organisation to go far beyond that.

Culture can enable success but can also block it or keep things status quo. In this chapter you'll learn how to overcome organisation inertia and change culture by working on the Heartset, Mindset and Actionset.

CHAPTER IN BRIEF

THE POWER QUESTION

How do you start changing behaviours?

THE PROBLEM

Culture is so powerful that it can cause you to fail or succeed. Also in the context of transformation culture is an extremely challenging topic and takes a lot of effort.

THE SOLUTION

Address Heartset, Mindset and Actionset. Together they make culture change.

THE REWARD

Doing this well creates a unique identity, a sense of purpose and belonging. It will make you a magnet for talent and leaders that you need to become successful. It will determine and activate your culture.

9.1 BARRIERS TO TRANSFORMATION

There are many barriers to transformation. You probably have encountered some of them in your daily life. Both at home and at work. In some aspects of life and work, you probably have been confronted with organisational inertia. It's what happens when established companies or organisations stick to old habits, become rigid in their thinking and actions, and lose track of the goal.

Fixing organisation inertia is not an easy task. You'll need to address not only leadership and systems but also the culture. If you don't, efforts to eliminate other barriers will have limited effect. People will go back to their routines, old habits and behaviours regardless of whether you asked them to transform. But beware, addressing behaviour and mindset will demand perseverance, smart efforts and special attention.

Culture is the way you do things in your company, in your community.

When sharing this with Stijn Nauwelaerts, Corporate Vice-President HR at Microsoft, he told us: "Culture is what you are creating together, it's the way your teams and stakeholders will be defining your organisation. The most important task here is closing the gap between the aspired culture and the lived experience of your team, your stakeholders, and the people who are closest to you. This work needs to be done every day, and it will never be fully completed."

Shockingly research from Gartner shows that 69% of employees don't believe in the cultural goals set by their leaders, 87% don't understand them, and 90% don't behave in ways that align with them.[45] Only 31% of HR leaders believe their organisations have the culture necessary to drive performance.[46]

The NeuroLeadership Institute, who study how the brain works in order to make organisations more human, studied why large culture change initiatives fail.[47]

"The biggest factor in why organisational change fails, involves a failure to change human habits. In case after case, everything was right – the strategy, the plans, the budget – but the people were not changing."
– The NeuroLeadership Institute.

So how do you build the desired company culture and get people to buy into it? How do you change the behaviours that underpin your desired organisational culture?

Barriers to transformation:

- ☑ Many management layers
- ☑ Politics, siloes and tunnel vision
- ☑ Lack of North Star
- ☑ No aligned culture
- ☑ Weak leadership and innovation skills
- ☑ Fear of failure
- ☑ Organisational inertia
- ☑ Weak execution
- ☑ Blind for the future
- ☑ Analysis paralysis
- ☑ Lack of budget and resources
- ☑ Legacy
- ☑ Risk aversity, compliancy and legal boundaries
- ☑ No time or prioritisation

9.2 ADDRESS THE HEARTSET, MINDSET AND ACTIONSET

As explained in Chapter 7 Anatomy of a Transformer, to succeed in your endeavours you will need to align what you say, how you behave and how you operate.

Culture is like the wind when climbing mountains. It is felt but not really visible. With the wind at your back, it will be easier to reach your North Star. With headwind, you may need to stop, return or change plans, slowing down your journey.

Culture change is not a top-down exercise. It affects the hearts, minds and habits of people.

You'll need to work also from the bottom up. From the inside-out.

To facilitate culture change, we've broken it down into three elements you'll need to address to change culture. We call it the Heartset, Mindset and Actionset of your people.

A. **Heartset** is the set of emotions, passions, fears and hopes that define how you see, feel and understand the world around you. It defines how you empathise with others. It's how you find hope, inspiration and excitement. It's your internal drive.

B. **Mindset** is the established set of attitudes, perceptions and beliefs shaping how you make sense of yourself, your life and the world around you. It influences how you think and behave. These are your belief systems.

C. **Actionset** is the set of behaviours and actions that will drive outcomes. These behaviours are defined by the values and norms of your culture.

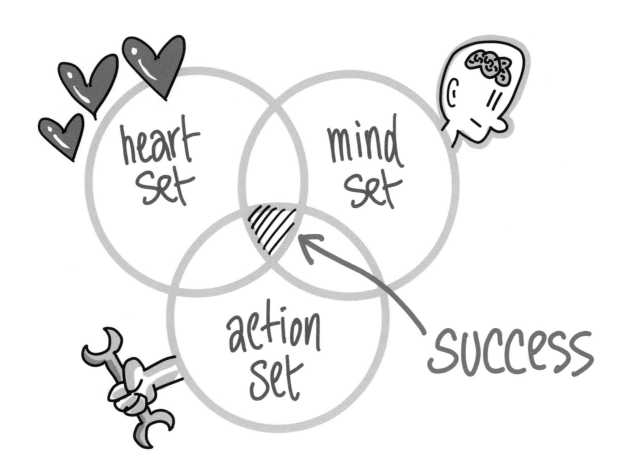

A. Heartset

What comes to mind when you think about Heartset? What images or thoughts pop up?

If Mindset is a frame of mind, an established set of attitudes, often linked to social or cultural values, then Heartset can be defined as a frame of heart. Heartset is much deeper seated. It is like an internal drive to achieving something. Failure leaves the heart unfulfilled, incomplete. It connects us to our core values, our why. Both are equally important in your journey to success.

If you want to change culture, you have to understand the Heartset of your people. Capture it. Touch it.

The question is how? How do you touch people's heart before you reach their head to get them on board.

STEPS

Step 1: Inspire people with a desirable future

☑ Frame your future North Star. Inspire with a clear story and give context so people understand the why. Do this in an authentic and empathic way. Let them digest it, comment on it, add to it.

☑ Help people imagine the future. Focus on what they want to achieve and what you need for that. Let them react on it. What do they want to add? Are they in agreement?

☑ Let them think about the impact, the value for them, but also for the organisation and for our ecosystem/society. It needs to be more compelling than the status quo. Let them think about the impact of doing nothing. Address the culture you need to make that future happen.

Step 2: Understand their emotions, passions, fears and hopes

☑ What are the current hopes and fears?

☑ Do they feel the future North Star is addressing those?

☑ Ask how satisfied they are with the current culture. If they are too satisfied they might not be willing to change.

Step 3: Address the possible tensions

☑ No friction usually means nothing is changing.

☑ Look for the detractors, the ones resisting most. They often indicate where the dominant culture is that may need to evolve.[48]

Step 4: Act as field journalist

☑ Report on the steps you are making, keep people posted on what is working and not working.

☑ Show practical examples of positive change and impact.

☑ Make it inspiring.

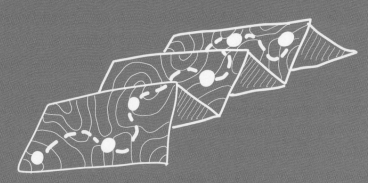

B. Mindset

Do you know what the dominant mindset is in your organisation and teams? Does it support the culture you need to be successful? Is it agile, collaborative? Is it one of abundance? Is it positive or negative? Are you dealing with a fixed or a growth mindset?

As discussed in Chapter 7, mindset drives behaviour, behaviour drives culture, and culture drives business outcomes.

Mindset is an important part of culture and defines a set of personal beliefs. Our mindset impacts how we behave, act and how we do things aligned with our own beliefs and understanding of, for example, the culture. It is sometimes referred to as your own truth.

Mindset usually sits on the individual level, but we could think of an organisational culture as a reflection of a collective mindset.

The growth mindset described by Carol Dweck at the Growth Mindset Institute[49] (see also Chapter 7) proposes a different way of viewing challenges and setbacks. Instead of seeing challenges and setbacks as blockers, people with a growth mindset, believe the setback is an opportunity, a necessary step that helps them grow and develop over time.

People with a growth mindset are more open, eager to learn and love challenges. In contrast, people with a fixed mindset, believe you can't change and prefer to focus on what they know. The good news is that you can develop your mindset into one of growth.

By its very nature, the journey of someone with a growth mindset is never finished.

"A growth mindset is the understanding that we can develop our abilities and intelligence. Research has shown that our implicit beliefs about the nature of intelligence can have a great impact on our achievement."

– Carol Dweck

STEPS TO DEVELOP A GROWTH MINDSET

Step 1: Let people discover their own mindset

☑ Let people discover their individual mindset. Make them self-reflect to become self-aware.

☑ Leverage scenario-based questions to figure out if someone is leaning more to a fixed or growth mindset.

☑ You can use the growth mindset development profiler (MDP).[50]

Step 2: Identify the collective mindset in your organisation

☑ Find out if your organisation has a dominant collective mindset.

☑ Leverage surveys, everyday observations, conversations.

☑ You can use the growth mindset development profiler (MDP) to assess your leaders and your organisation. Is it a fixed or growth mindset? Explain the difference and the value for the organisation.

Step 3: Agree on your journey

☑ Find your coalition of the willing. Ask who wants to actively participate in the culture change.

☑ These people will help you capture the hearts and minds of people and enable change.

☑ They become your ambassadors to start the movement of changing the culture.

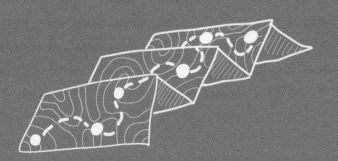

C. Actionset

After addressing Heartset and Mindset it is time to act.

How can your organisation shift the mindset of your people and develop the behavioural expectations to bring its culture to life? What do you need to make it easier for people to do something different? How do you keep the culture and the new behaviours/habits alive?

The coalition of the willing, identified in the previous section, can work out the next steps.

There are five areas you will want to keep in mind to strengthen the desired behaviours, as listed on the next page.

Now you must bring the new ambitions and culture to life in real-life habits and behaviours. Do this one at a time allowing people to build those new habits without being overwhelmed or confused.

One of our customers asked us, "Who owns culture?" We believe that everyone collectively owns culture and actively participates in shaping and nurturing it. However, to build it or change it in a company or organisational setting, the leadership should kick-start it, shape it and cultivate it involving everyone. Whether you design or develop culture or not, it will grow anyway, like a weed. But a weed may prevent other plants growing.

Areas to strengthen the desired behaviours

Areas	What you need to put in place to strengthen the desired behaviours
1. Behaviours	An actionable set of expected behavioural patterns and habits you want behind the values and norms. Need to be co-created, validated with your teams and rolled-out in the organisation through supporting programmes one at a time.
2. Systems	Organisational processes, policies and tools, such as operating rhythms, scorecard, performance reviews, coaching sessions (the what and how are equally important), feedback processes, change programmes and listening systems that reinforce the culture.
3. Awards	The rewards (e.g. if one team is a desired value then you need to have x-team awards in place), incentives (both team and individual) and recognition to reward the right behaviours.
4. Symbols and Artefacts	Use symbols and artefacts in rituals, stories, visuals and language to bring your culture to life to make it tangible. For instance, how you run off-sites, onboard people, have parties, give away awards. Think of how you tell stories of your heritage. Use visuals to create an identity on the walls, in the office, online, using mascots, T-shirts, stickers, roll up flags etc.
5. Personal Stories	Enable everyone to tell the story of your culture through their actions, events, meetings, and communication. Let them become great storytellers and show examples of how they brought the culture to life.

EXAMPLE UMICORE

The Umicore Way and the importance of culture

Two decades ago, Umicore was a classic, old-school smelting company. Today, as a pioneering recycler of waste metals, it is at the cutting edge of the so-called circular economy, refining, recycling and manufacturing specialised products from precious metals, cobalt, germanium, zinc and other metals.

Umicore's transformation is a story of radically changing business models and total dedication to developing new technologies. But also one of people and culture. Their organisational values are the compass that keeps everyone on course. They are not just words on paper, they are actually lived by senior management. The values of openness, innovation, respect, teamwork and commitment are crucial to Umicore's success. They promote these values and address deficiencies in an appropriate way.

"The Umicore Way is the cornerstone of everything we do at Umicore. It outlines our values and the way in which we wish to achieve our strategy and our overall commitment to the principles of sustainable development. The Umicore Way is not only for Umicore employees but also covers our relationships with all our stakeholders. Our ultimate aim is that by living The Umicore Way we will become an even more successful and respected company."[52]

(from The Umicore Way)

9.3 BUILD YOUR OWN CULTURE PROGRAMME

Align employees to your culture by making sure they know what culture you aspire to and why you need it to succeed. Engage and co-create the details with them. They need to believe in the culture and understand what behaviours will support that culture.

Follow these three steps to build your own programmes helping you break undesirable organisational habits and encourage new behaviours.

STEPS

Step 1: Specify the desired culture (North Star exercise)

☑ Culture is one of the North Star pillars where you answer the questions: What culture (values/norms) do you need to succeed? What do you keep and what do you need to develop?

☑ Follow the steps in The North Star Chapter 2 on how you can determine your desired culture.

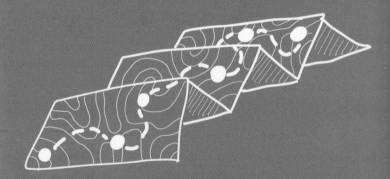

Step 2: Identify the behaviours for each of the values

- ☑ List the desired behaviours (actionable set of expected behavioural patterns) behind each of them (max three per value).

- ☑ Complete the two sentences: "Wouldn't it be great if we…" (which surfaces the behaviours) and "But we don't because…" (which helps pinpoint the blockers).

- ☑ Uncover them through workshops, surveys, world cafés, interviews, co-creation or day in the life journals.

Step 3: Come up with specific interventions and programmes

- ☑ Use a simple template like the below examples where the group specifies the behaviours sought, the habits blocking them and determines the solution/programme (enablers, nudges, tools, systems, processes, storytelling) that would help employees break through them and promote change through reinforcement.

- ☑ Vote on the most relevant ones.

- ☑ Deploy them one by one in a fun and inspiring way.

- ☑ Learn and reimagine where needed.

EXAMPLES PROGRAMMES

Below you'll find inspiration from a couple of real-life programme examples to make it tangible[51]:

DBS, the Development Bank of Singapore Limited

Culture goal
Decisive and purpose-driven

Challenge
Dysfunctional meetings as a major blocker that entrenched organisational inertia and hindered innovation. DBS was nicknamed "Damned Bloody Slow".

Title programme
MOJO

Goal
Promote efficient, effective, open, and collaborative meetings.

Solution
Research at Google showed that equal share of voice and psychological safety were critical to high-performing, highly innovative project teams. So DBS assigned in every meeting an MO, a Meeting Owner, who sets a clear agenda, with an agreed start and end, and who ensures all attendees are given an equal say. And every meeting also had a JO, a Joyful Observer, who makes sure the meeting was run crisply, encourages broad inclusive participation and gives feedback to the MO. The MO had the authority to call for a "phone Jenga" for instance for all attendees to put their phones in a pile on the table (like the game Jenga).

Result
Meetings at DBS no longer run late, are more effective, open and collaborative, having saved an estimated 500,000 employee hours to date.

Atlassian, an Australian software company

Culture goal
Impactful

Challenge
Critical voices not being heard when starting new projects.

Title programme
PREMORTEM.

Goal
Identify threats to new initiatives and develop a defence against them.

Solution
Before starting a project, teams meet to discuss how it could fail, doing a seven-step exercise that includes a structured cross-examination (in which a group arguing the "success" case questions a group arguing the "failure" case and vice versa), voting to gauge risk severity, assigning risk "owners", and planning how to minimise threats.

Result
Increased their success rates substantially.

"The easiest way to change people's behaviour is to change their environment."

- Daniel Kahneman, Nobel Prize winner known for his work on behavioural economics, explains how it is important to create the conditions that facilitates the desired behaviour to emerge in a natural way. He calls it the human way which in many situations is a stronger alternative to incentives.

There are many other exercises (of the heart) that we introduced during Chapter 2 The North Star and Chapter 5 Align, Amplify and Act that also can help you change behaviours:

a. Guardian and the Footprint : probe for individual purpose. It's a great empathy exercise and paves the way for alignment. as speed date.

b. Fishbowl on culture: create a safe environment to share and have generative conversations on culture.

c. Newcomers on stage sharing their observations of the current culture: a fresh view on culture from recent hires.

d. Everyone is an innovator exercise to show everyone can innovate: run small exercises so people learn to combine ideas and understand there is an innovator in each of us.

e. "What will our stakeholders say in the future?" (quotes)

What you have learned...

Activating and living your culture will demand perseverance, smart efforts and special attention to people across the organisation to get things done. The key is to update them on the big picture and let them work out what this means to them, how they can be part of it and what has to happen to make it successful.

To overcome organisational inertia and change culture you will need to work on Heartset, Mindset and Actionset.

☑ **Heartset** is the set of emotions, passions, fears and hopes that define how you see, feel and understand the world around you.

☑ **Mindset** is the established set of attitudes, perceptions and beliefs shaping how you make sense of yourself, your life and the world around you.

☑ **Actionset** is the set of behaviours and actions that will drive outcomes.

Culture change is not a top-down exercise. It affects the hearts, minds and habits of people.

BRINGING IT ALL TOGETHER

REAL-LIFE CASES

The book offers a simple but effective approach for organisations to Transform and Perform.

It all starts with alignment on context and problems using a Power Question and then defining the North Star by answering four key questions about purpose, future success, value for stakeholders, and culture. Actionable insights are then gathered through a deep dive into the current reality, and transformation areas are clustered into big themes. The flow and tools of part one help you document your journey, challenge yourself along the way and stay the course.

Part two is all about getting to action and getting everyone on board. Building the bridge and expanding it will amplify the effects and create a lasting impact. A typical process of transformation spans three stages: align, amplify, and act. Applying the Power of 3, i.e. combining visualisation, inspiration, and co-creation, in each of those stages helps create conditions for group genius to emerge and accelerates the outcome.

Part three dives into personal, business and culture aspects of transformation. Start with yourself with twelve principles for personal transformation. Get inspired by organisations that turned transformation into a strategic capability, the gift that keeps giving.

The concepts and ideas presented in this book only have value if they help solve your problems and generate value for you and your teams. You will be the judge of that, but we wanted to give you a taste of what it looks like when they are brought to live and applied in real-world scenarios. To that purpose, we curated a collection of business cases that demonstrate how to use the concepts. In this we attempt to address the different stages, being align, amplify and act.

Showcasing these business cases meant we had to proceed with caution, given the confidentiality of the information shared. We asked for approval to ensure we did not compromise any sensitive information or breach any non-disclosure agreements. We understand some things had to be blanked out or couldn't be shown at all, but still would like to express our gratitude to all customers who collaborated on the business cases here and throughout the book.

We hope that these cases will inspire you to try out some of our concepts and tools, and they help you in developing new ideas and insights for your own business.

So, sit back, and enjoy the journey as we bring the chapters of this book to life in a practical way through those real-world examples.

The business cases presented are:

STAGES 1, 2 and 3: ALIGN, AMPLIFY and ACT with SES, a global leading satellite operator.

STAGE 1: ALIGN with the Joint Research Center (JRC) of the European Commission and the startup Swoove Studio, trade name of Intelligent Internet Machines BV.

STAGE 3: ACT with Torfs, a Belgian shoe retailer.

The 3 stages

	Align	Amplify	Act
Typical audience	**Core team** e.g. leadership team, management team, core project team, transformation lead team	**Key stakeholders, often internal, and influencers** e.g. extended leadership, managers, key stakeholders, key talent	**All other impacted** e.g. managers, experts, business units, all employees, external stakeholders
Objectives	**Aligning on the key components of the journey** • Find the North Star • Asses your current reality • Create your Bridge	**Amplifying and multiplying the impact** • Validate the North Star • Deep dive on culture and behaviours • Co-create detailed Bridge initiatives and prioritise	**Activating the plan and acting accordingly** • Implement North Star • Translate the Bridge priorities into projects or sprints • Iterate, learn and adapt
Formats	Off-sites 1 or 2 days	Off-sites 1 or more days	• Power Teams (virtual teams) • Pitch Days • Specific business unit deep dives • Employee days • Stakeholder roadshows
Typical audience size	5-15	20-150	Any size
Time to completion	2-3 months	2-3 months	Minimum 3 months

BUSINESS CASE STAGE 1-2-3:
SES, A LEADING GLOBAL SATELLITE OPERATOR

Company snapshot

SES, Société Européenne des Satellites, was founded in 1985 as Europe's first private satellite operator with the strong support of the Luxembourg government who remained a major shareholder. Today it is a global satellite telecommunications network provider supplying video and data connectivity worldwide to broadcasters, content and internet service providers, mobile and fixed network operators, governments and institutions. SES is one of the world's leading satellite owners and operators with over 70 satellites in two different orbits, geostationary orbit (GEO) and medium Earth orbit (MEO).

Revenue in 2021: 1.8B Euro with 2060 employees

The starting point

CEO Steve Collar and HR director Evie Roos contacted us to help them in their transformation to respond to the major disruptions happening in their market.

STAGE 1: ALIGN with core leadership

1. THE POWER QUESTION

The Senior Leadership Team (SLT) met face to face for a Strategic Off-Site. The power question of that session was "What is the strategic direction and transformative culture that will deliver top stakeholder value and exponential success for SES+?"

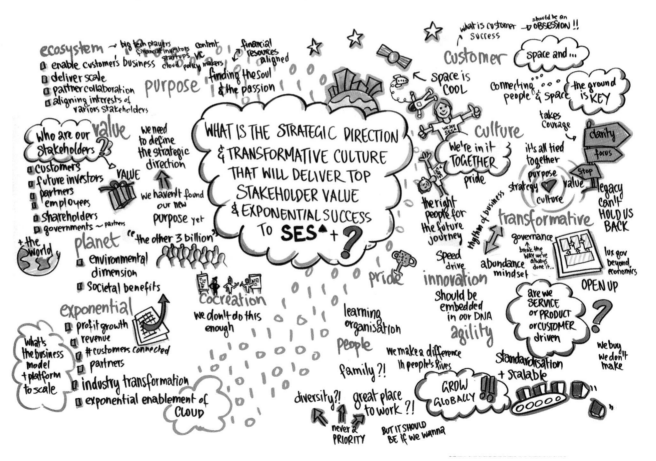

2. THE NORTH STAR

We do the
EXTRAORDINARY
in SPACE

to deliver
AMAZING
EXPERIENCES

EVERYWHERE
on EARTH

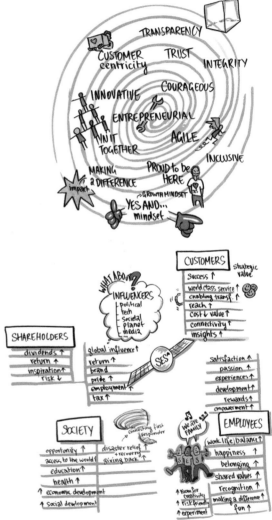

TRANSPARENCY

CUSTOMER centricity · TRUST · INTEGRITY

INNOVATIVE · COURAGEOUS

ENTREPRENEURIAL

IN IT TOGETHER · AGILE

INCLUSIVE

MAKING a DIFFERENCE · PROUD to be HERE

impact

GROWTH MINDSET

YES AND... mindset

AMBITIONS

← North Star

space is COOL

Let's make a dent in the UNIVERSE

We believe in CONTENT & CONNECTIVITY everywhere

We are the leading cloud-enabled satellite based INTELLIGENT CONNECTIVITY provider

We are FUTURE PROOF powered by SUSTAINABLE GROWTH & INNOVATION

We are passionate about CUSTOMER EXPERIENCE & focused on CUSTOMER SUCCESS

VALUE

SES is a GREAT PLACE to WORK

family

We're in it TOGETHER

We are here to MAKE a DIFFERENCE

WHAT ABOUT?

INFLUENCERS
- political
- tech
- societal
- planet
- media

CUSTOMERS

Strategic value

Success ↑
World class service ↑
enabling transf. ↑
reach ↑
cost & value ↑
connectivity ↑
insights ↑

SHAREHOLDERS

dividends ↑
return ↑
inspiration ↑
risk ↓

global influence ↑
return ↑
brand
pride ↑
employment ↑
tax ↑

SES

satisfaction ↑
passion ↑
experiences ↑
development ↑
rewards ↑
empowerment ↑

SOCIETY

connecting first responders

We are family

EMPLOYEES

opportunity ↑
access to the world ↑
education ↑
health ↑
↑ economic development
↑ social development

disaster relief + recovery
giving back

↑ room for creativity
↑ risk friendly
↑ experiment

work life balance ↑
happiness ↑
belonging ↑
shared values ↑
recognition ↑
making a difference ↑
fun ↑

3. THE CURRENT REALITY

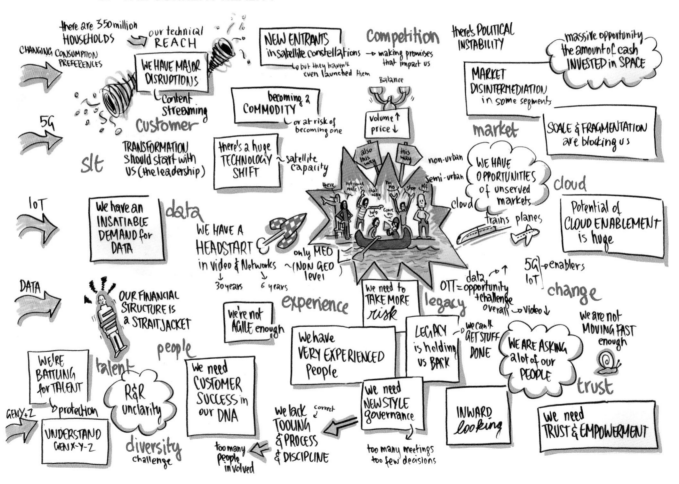

there are 350 million HOUSEHOLDS

our technical REACH

CHANGING CONSUMPTION PREFERENCES

WE HAVE MAJOR DISRUPTIONS

Content Streaming

Customer

5G

slt

TRANSFORMATION should start with US (the leadership)

NEW ENTRANTS in satellite constellations → making promises that impact us
↳ but they haven't even launched them

Competition

becoming a COMMODITY
↳ or at risk of becoming one

there's a huge TECHNOLOGY SHIFT ~ satellite capacity

there's POLITICAL INSTABILITY

massive opportunity the amount of cash INVESTED in SPACE

MARKET DISINTERMEDIATION in some segments

market

SCALE & FRAGMENTATION are blocking us

Balance

Volume ↑ price ↓

also this way / this way

non-urban

semi-urban

WE HAVE OPPORTUNITIES of unserved markets

cloud

IoT

We have an INSATIABLE DEMAND for DATA

data

WE HAVE A HEADSTART
in video & Networks
↓ 30 years / 6 years

only MEO ~ (NON GEO level

cloud

trains   planes

Potential of CLOUD ENABLEMENT is huge

DATA

OUR FINANCIAL STRUCTURE is a STRAITJACKET

We're not AGILE enough

experience

we need to TAKE MORE risk

OTT = opportunity + challenge overall → video ↓

data ↗ ↑

legacy

5G → enablers
IoT

change

LEGACY is holding us BACK

We can't GET STUFF DONE

we are not MOVING FAST enough

WE ARE ASKING a lot of our PEOPLE

trust

people

talent

WE'RE BATTLING for TALENT

GEN Y+Z ↳ protection

UNDERSTAND GEN X-Y-Z

R&R unclarity

We need CUSTOMER SUCCESS in our DNA

We have VERY EXPERIENCED People

We need NEW STYLE governance

INWARD looking

We need TRUST & EMPOWERMENT

diversity challenge

We lack TOOLING & PROCESS & DISCIPLINE

correct

too many people involved

too many meetings too few decisions

4. THE BRIDGE

The details of the actions taken for each strategic theme are not provided due to confidentiality reasons.

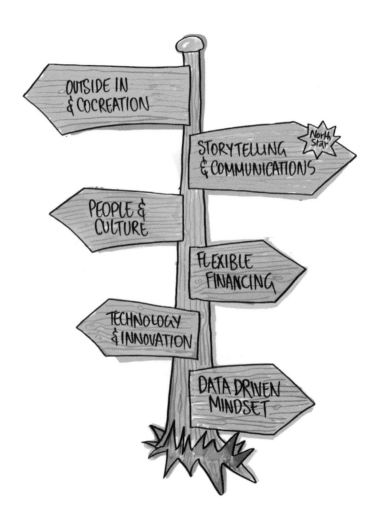

5. THE END RESULT

The result at the end of the session was a visual summary of the entire strategy, from the problems in the current state to success in the future state and the bridge with strategic themes and initiatives needed to make it reality.

STAGE 2: AMPLIFY with top 100 global leaders

After the strategy off site, we helped the client organise a 3-day global SES conference in Berlin for their top 100 global leaders. To increase focus and create a buzz for the event, we came up with 3 leading themes 'Re-imagine, Connect and Act'. The entire event was built up around these leading themes.

We started by landing the new future-proof North Star developed with the senior leadership team, with its purpose 'We do the extraordinary in space, to deliver the amazing experiences everywhere on earth'. Through a series of inspiring keynotes with internal and external speakers (customers, tech companies,

newcomers, project owners) and co-creation workshops engaging everyone in the room, we reflected on the why, what and how of personal and business transformation. We visualised the current state, the desired future state, looking forward 5 years from now, and detailed the bridge listing strategic initiatives and priorities for the next 12 months. The whole process was visually facilitated resulting in a large mural that is now on display in the SES offices. We also took our time to dive deeper into the culture.

1. THE CULTURE FISHBOWL

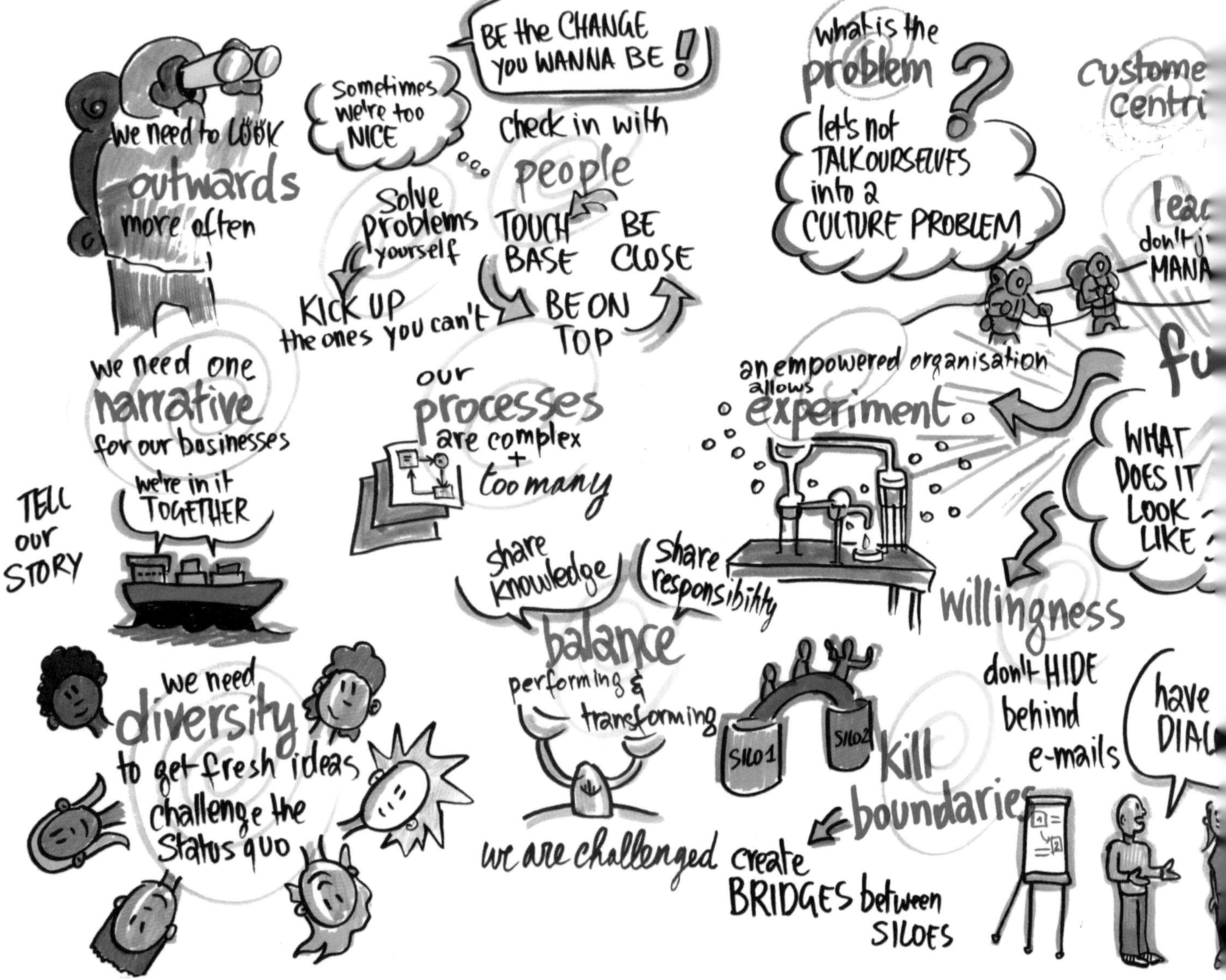

BERLIN 2019
SES
RE-IMAGINE...
CONNECT
ACT!
BERLIN 2019
TRANSFORMATION at MICROSOFT
GROWTH mindset
performing while transforming
transform yourself before you transform others !!

2. THE EXPERIENCE

To make it a unique experience, we co-created event branding artifacts including logos, flyers and banners to engage participants before, during and after the event. The theme visual shows a diverse team co-creating things that will impact the world, but also space, which is their core business. The same themes and visual elements were used for invitation e-mails, event communication, badges and welcome signs. On the day of the event, a massive roll-up was inviting everyone in from the moment they set foot in the venue.

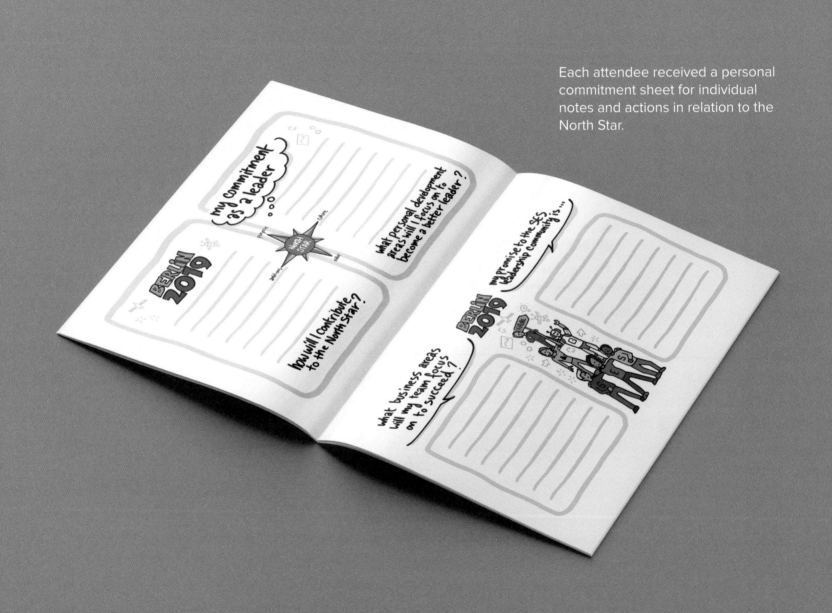

Each attendee received a personal commitment sheet for individual notes and actions in relation to the North Star.

Besides mentioning name and role,
the badges and lanyards helped
attendees find their way to their
teams and break-out sessions.

STAGE 3: ACT with all stakeholders

At the close of the Berlin conference, we created power teams by asking each attendee to select the ambition they wanted to continue working on after the event. Many of the co-creation outcomes and priorities became projects. So we organised Pitch Days, to help them pitch their projects within each ambition. We conducted business unit deep dives with specific teams, such as the sales teams, technology teams, and the board of directors. They launched an innovation lab, called L-192, and established a global cloud strategy.

BUSINESS CASE STAGE 1: ALIGN WITH THE JOINT RESEARCH CENTER (JRC), EUROPEAN COMMISSION

Company profile

The Joint Research Centre (JRC) is a source of scientific and technical reference for policy-makers. It serves the European Commission and also works closely with the EU Member States, the European Parliament, the Council and other institutions. It has more than 2300 scientists and supporting staff working with more than 1000 public and private organisations. The Joint Research Centre (JRC) provides independent, evidence-based knowledge and science supporting European Union (EU) policies to positively impact society.

The starting point

We were contacted by Stephen Quest, Director-General of the JRC, who at the time was just appointed as new leader of the JRC. He asked us to help him re-imagine the JRC and support them in their transformation.

1. THE POWER QUESTION

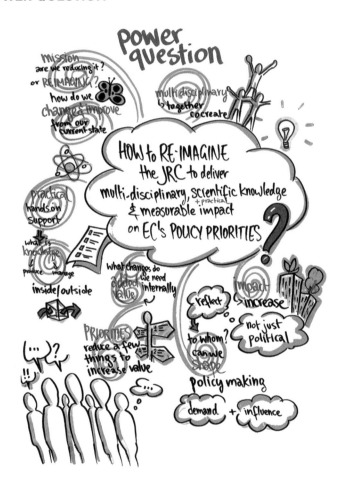

2. THE NORTH STAR

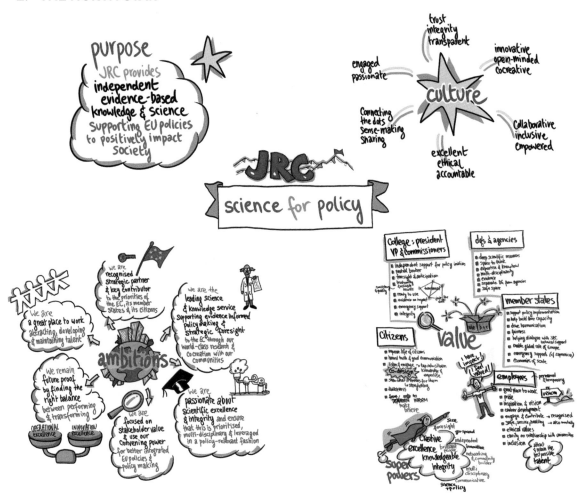

3. THE NORTH STAR TRANSLATION IN OFFICIAL EC JRC DOCUMENTS

The JRC published a revitalisation of its Strategy 2030 to strengthen their role at the service of the European project. They leveraged the North Star in their official publication of their 2030 strategy.

The full document 'Revitalising the JRC strategy 2030' is publicly available on the website of the Publications Office of the European Union.

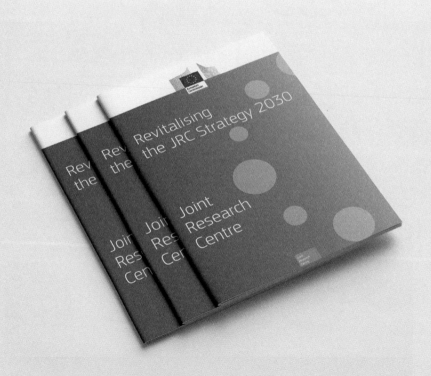

By revitalising our Strategy 2030
and ambitions, ...

Our ambitions for the future of the JRC can only be fully realised if they are embedded in the culture of our organisation. The way we carry out our work is as important as the work itself, and this is represented in our core values.

We are a people-centric organisation and the values set out in the Strategy 2030 remain as true as ever. As part of our North Star process of positioning the JRC, we re-evaluated these of integrity, accountability, openness, innovation and inclusiveness. We re-evaluated these and established a broadened set of values to help us define the culture we want to encourage. During discussions and consultations across the JRC, three core values were identified which JRC staff most wished to see enacted in their working lives now. These three core values will drive our efforts as we seek to transform the way we work in the coming period.

Trust, collaboration and transparency are mutually reinforcing and represent the way we want to work with each other, and the reputation we want to build for ourselves externally.

TRUST

Inside the JRC, our successful Trust Pilot will be rolled out across the organisation to trigger more conversations on the nature of trust and how it can be nurtured in our working relationships.

Looking outwards, the JRC will maintain and enhance its reputation for producing robust scientific evidence as a trusted partner for policymakers.

COLLABORATION

Inside the JRC, our new portfolio way of working will encompass staff at all levels to collaborate routinely, where and across portfolio, creating a new, integrated view across the policy areas we address.

Looking outwards, we will enhance new partnerships across Europe and internationally to broaden the knowledge base and reach of our work.

TRANSPARENCY

Inside the JRC, management will continue to model transparency by sharing progress and seeking views, recognising that our shared journey is strengthened by a common sense of purpose.

Looking outwards, the JRC practices open science, making its findings and data sets publicly available where possible for maximum impact and accountability.

Moreover, we will prioritise investment in specific human resources policies in line with our ambition to be a great place to work.

By revitalising our Strategy 2030, we are setting our North Star: our purpose and ambitions, our culture and values, and the offer we make to our partners in the European Commission and beyond (our value proposition).

OUR PURPOSE

The JRC provides independent, evidence-based knowledge and science, supporting EU policies to positively impact society.

OUR AMBITIONS

We are recognised as a strategic partner and key contributor to the priorities of the European Commission, Member States and citizens.

We are the leading science and knowledge service, supporting evidence-informed policymaking and strategic foresight through our world-class research and co-creation with (partner) communities.

We are a great place to work, attracting, developing and maintaining talent.

We are passionate about scientific excellence and integrity, and ensure that this is prioritised, multi-disciplinary and leveraged in a policy-relevant fashion.

We remain future-proof by finding the right balance between performing (operational excellence) and transforming (innovation excellence).

We are focused on stakeholder value and use our convening power for better integrated EU policies and policymaking.

9

BUSINESS CASE STAGE 1: ALIGN WITH THE SWOOVE STUDIO, TRADE NAME OF INTELLIGENT INTERNET MACHINES BV, A 3D ANIMATION START-UP

Company profile

Start-up Swoove Studio has the ambition to democratise 3D animation. They have developed Swoove Studio for this purpose, a mobile app with which everyone can easily create stories with 3D animated characters and then share them on their social media, such as TikTok, Instagram or YouTube.

1. THE POWER QUESTION

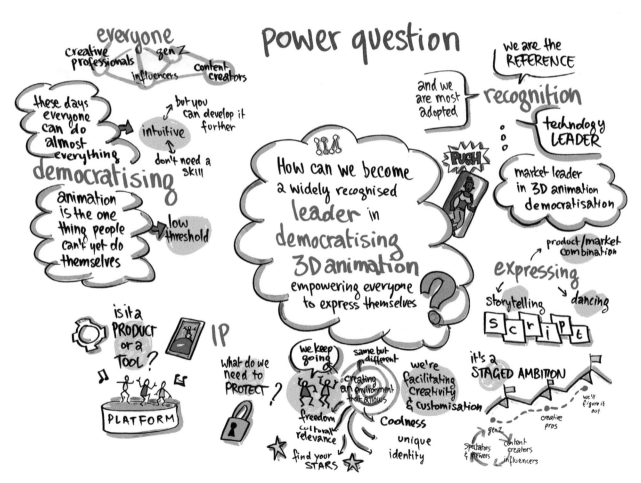

purpose ☆

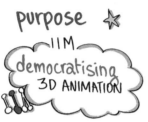

IIM
democratising
3D ANIMATION

culture ☆

ENTREPRENEURIAL & INNOVATIVE

AGILE

OPEN MINDED

USER EXPERIENCE driven

INTEGRITY

RESULT DRIVEN

CUTTING EDGE

WIN-WIN

ambitions ☆

We are WIDELY RECOGNISED for DEMOCRATISING 3D ANIMATION

We are the #1 REALTIME & EASY TO USE PLATFORM & TOOL for 3D animation

We are the COOLEST 3D-animation app for everyone

Our balance between PERFORMING & TRANSFORMING creates HAPPY PARTNERS & SHAREHOLDERS

We put RESPECT & INTEGRITY at the HEART of our COMPANY

We are a GREAT PLACE to WORK powered by happy & diverse TALENT

☆ value

I can express myself creatively

"USERS"
- exposure ↑
- influence ↑
- recognition ↑
- respect ↑
- expression ↑
- engagement ↑
- fun ↑
- coolness ↑
- bragging value ↑ rights
- views ↑
- reach ↑
- community ↑ ~ sense of belonging

"BRANDS"
- reach ↑ visibility ↑
- engagement ↑
- gateway to gen Z ↑ access
- reputation ↑
- community ↑
- revenue ↑

"SHAREHOLDERS"
- return ↑ value creation financial
- pride ↑
- satisfaction ↑
- learning ↑
- transparency ↑
- (accountability ↑)
- sustainability ↑ ~ sustainable returns

WE trust 'm!

reputation is key!!

"CONTENT SUPPLIERS"
dancers
characters
props
music
backgrounds
clothing
accessories
- audience ↑
- extra outlet / distribution channel
- revenue ↑
- exposure ↑
- recognition ↑
- marketing ↑

"EMPLOYEES"
- personal growth ↑%
- fun fun fun ↑ diversity
- engagement ↑ passion↑
- pride ↑ health ↑
- attrition↓ loyalty ↑
- team spirit ↑ | rewards↑
- energy ↑ | motivation ↑

RESPECT

appreciation !! financial status

"INFLUENCERS"
- fame ↑
- belonging ↑
- exposure ↑ extra reach ↑
- uniqueness | differentiation ↑
- revenue ↑
- collaboration ↑
- networking ↑

3. THE CURRENT STATE

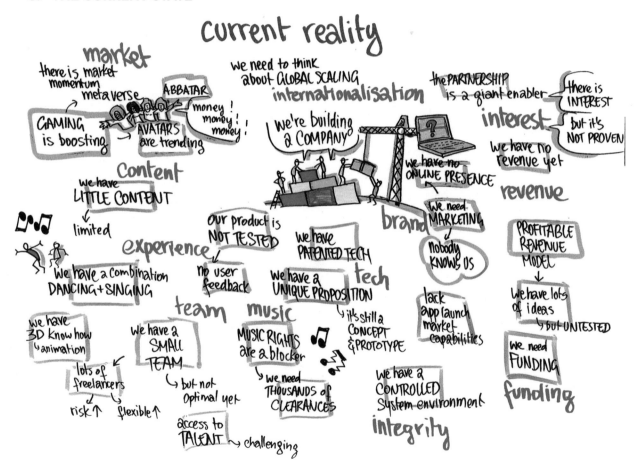

4. THE BRIDGE

bridge

let's PUSH this forward !!

observe users

NORTH STAR

- Create Communication package to TRANSLATE AMBITIONS/NORTH STAR for INTERNAL/EXTERNAL USE. *incl. PURPOSE CULTURE*
- agree how we LAND this with the TEAM
- do something to bring the team together
- keep shareholders involved
- detail desired behaviours behind culture (6-9 months + in cocreation)

PROBLEM-SOLUTION FIT

- understand + accelerate customer journey
- user testing prototype III
- acquire minimum {visual content / music
- revisit feature set MVP
- beef up social media + storytelling
- Legal Framework → commercial for {B2C / B2B

PRODUCT-MARKET FIT

- Showcase + test product
- market validation + testing at scale
- select & validate 3 B2B vertical partners → retail / music / fashion → sports
- prepare ROADSHOW for NEXT ROUND → seeding A
- on-board MARKETING + APP LAUNCH MUSCLE
- finalise launch partnership + sign
- Crystalise MUSIC offerings ↳ fix rights issues
- finalise MONETISATION strategy for first phase ↳ define next step
- get scalable infrastructure in place
- develop Contingency / plan B

let's launch this baby

SCALE FIT

- prepare INTERNATIONAL ROLL OUT
- define ORGANISATIONAL MODEL + REQUIRED CAPABILITIES
- define USER acquisition strategy
- expand the BOARD (~ seeding A) → other vertical PARTNER READY
- validate FINANCIAL ASSUMPTIONS → through partnership

BUSINESS CASE STAGE 3: ACT WITH TORFS, A BELGIAN SHOE RETAILER

Company profile

Torfs is a Belgian family-owned shoe retailer. Founded in 1948, the company has grown to become one of the largest shoe retailers in Belgium, and has won the Best Employer award as a Great Place to Work in Belgium 10 times, as well as the European edition in 2019. It is well-know for its investment in people and its culture.

Below shows how Torfs leveraged the work they did on the North Star for their employee days as part of their amplify and act stage. This is translated from the Dutch original.

THE POWER TEST

To help you assess your progress on transforming while performing, we've included forty hopefully thought-provoking questions.

These forty questions delve into different aspects of the nine chapters in the book. By reflecting on your responses to these questions, you can evaluate your progress towards transformational goals and identify areas for improvement.

Whether you're an individual seeking personal growth or a leader looking to transform your organisation, this Power Test will provide you with a practical framework for self-assessment and reflection.

So, let's explore these forty questions and embark on a journey towards finding balance in Transforming while Performing.

THE POWER QUESTIONS

1. We know what problem(s) we are trying to solve.

THE NORTH STAR

2. We know why we exist. Our purpose is clearly articulated.

3. We know what our future success looks like. Our ambitions are known and shared.

4. We know what value we want to create for your stakeholders. Our value proposition is known and shared.

5. We know what culture will help us realise our North Star. Our culture and values are known and lived by everyone in our organisation.

THE CURRENT REALITY

6. We see what is happening inside and outside the company that can enable or block our future success.

7. We mapped the megatrends and understand its implications.

THE BRIDGE

8. We have an actionable and impactful plan that addresses the important themes and initiatives in line with our North Star.

ACT, AMPLIFY AND ACT

9. We put the right practices in place to align, amplify and act on our North Star and action plans.

THE POWER OF 3

10. We leverage the power of inspiration, visualisation and co-creation to spark imagination, maximise group genius and create lasting impact.

PERSONAL TRANSFORMATION

11. I don't let my ego get in the way.

12. My first answer is yes. I always look for possibilities and opportunities.

13. I do not worship any organisation, technology, product, service or business model.

14. I balance creativity, passion and wisdom (or experience).

15. I have an open mindset.

16. I am curious, dare to take risks and see failure as part of the journey to success.

17. I embrace diversity and inclusion.

18. I have aligned what I say, how I behave and how I operate.

19. I am trustworthy and I trust others.

20. I understand people make the company or organisation and that I am part of that.

21. I invest in and maintain personal relationships.

22. I am practising storytelling.

23. I started transforming myself before I expected others to transform.

BUSINESS TRANSFORMATION.

24. We are ready to reinvent ourselves by building a new North Star.

25. We have visionary and operational leaders at the top.

26. We created a capabilities-focused leadership model.

27. We have diverse leadership styles.

28. We balance an operating model for both running the day-to-day and transforming for the long term.

29. We mix the traditional R&D in products, services and technology with R&D in business model innovation.

30. We mix internal innovation and corporate venturing to fuel our innovation strategy.

31. We have a culture of trust.

32. We manage the tension between transforming and performing.

CULTURE TRANSFORMATION

33. We are addressing the heartset, mindset and actionset to enable culture change and break organisational inertia.

34. We understand the hopes and fears of our people.

35. We know what the collective mindset is in our organisation.

36. We have identified the coalition of the willing for the culture change.

37. We specified the desired culture.

38. We identified the behaviours for each of the values

39. We have established programs to enable the desired behaviours.

40. We also looked at our systems, awards, symbols, artifacts and personal stories.

LEXICON

- ☑ **Transforming while Performing:** finding balance in building your future while delivering on the day-to-day, mixing innovation with operational excellence.

- ☑ **Operational Excellence:** the area where you deliver on your commitments in the short(er) term. the process of making your day-to-day performance more efficient. It's where you grow the business, operate the supply chain, create cash, deliver on time, create return for shareholders and value for customers, where you develop your capabilities, where you improve profit margins, where you acquire a larger market share. Your focus here is on people, customers, profitability, and society... of today.

- ☑ **Innovation Excellence:** the area where you build your future in the long run. It is the power that drives you forward, the belief in your future. It is long term oriented. It is where you introduce radically new elements to your culture, organisation, products, services, customer relationships, business models and possibly even replace it by something superior. Your focus here is on people, customers, profit and the society... of tomorrow.

- ☑ **Power Question:** a question that describes what problem you are trying to solve. It helps you align, focus and make sure you solve the right problem. A power question is a powerful tool before starting any task, meeting or even making a decision.

- ☑ **North Star:** a compass that drives everyone forward and provides a common direction of travel that informs every action. It includes your purpose, your ambitions, the value for your stakeholders and your culture. This is about where are you going and why.

- ☑ **Current reality:** a clear picture of the biggest trends, challenges and opportunities, both from the inside-out as well as from the outside-in that can block or enable success. This is about where you are today.

- ☑ **Bridge:** an action plan with concrete initiatives that addresses your power question, your current reality and paves the way towards reaching your North Star. This is about how you get there.

☑ **Align, amplify and act:** the three stages of your transformation to address resistance and get people inspired and energised to start the journey. You start small with a core team to align on the key aspects of the North Star and strategy. As you progress in your transformation planning, the intention is to address a larger group of stakeholders to make the plan better and more tangible, more tactical. We call this the amplify stage. And lastly get things done in the act phase, where you multiply the effects of the transformation plan across the organisation and with your ecosystem. How do you create more impact?

☑ **Power of 3:** the combination of inspiration, visualisation and co-creation to let group genius emerge, spark imagination and to accelerate true transformation with lasting impact. This is how you get everyone on board to act in days, not months.

☑ **Inspiration:** inspire people and spark them into getting creative at the start of your transformation journey. Feeling inspired unlocks creativity, enhances productivity, and boosts happiness.

☑ **Visualisation:** any technique for creating images, diagrams, or animations to communicate a message. Graphic facilitation or visual facilitation is visually recording or facilitating your meetings and conferences on large murals. It stimulates group learning, increases participation and creates a collective memory of the event.

☑ **Co-creation:** is the process in which input from a broad group of stakeholders is solicited to create value. It is a collaborative approach that seeks to tap into the collective knowledge, creativity, and expertise of all participants to create something that is greater than the sum of its parts.

☑ **Power Teams:** virtual teams consisting of members of different units that will each work out in more detail the chosen transformation themes and refine the initiatives and actions that must be taken.

☑ **Pitch Days:** an exercise for team to evolve the projects, focus on their pitching and storytelling skills, priorities and asks. You brainstorm within a power team on a transformation initiative and prepare a 15-minute pitch, explaining the context, the problem, the solution, the value and the asks.

☑ **Personal Transformation:** transforming to secure future business success isn't just about re-imagining your company or your strategy, but also re-imagining yourself. How do you transform yourself first?

☑ **Business Transformation:** to become resilient as an organisation, to perform and to scale fast, you have to build in transformation as a strategic capability. How do you turn transforming into performing?

☑ **Culture Transformation:** address heartset, mindset and actionset to change and enable your culture. How do you start changing behaviours?

☑ **Heartset:** set of emotions, passions, fears, and hopes that define how you see, feel and understand the world around you. It defines how you empathise with others. It's how you find hope, inspiration and excitement. It's your internal drive.

☑ **Mindset:** the established set of attitudes, perceptions and beliefs shaping how you make sense of yourself, your life and the world around you. It influences how they think and behave. They are your belief systems.

☑ **Actionset:** the set of behaviours and actions that will drive outcomes. They are behaviours defined by the values and norms of your culture.

☑ **Visual Senseformers:** our name combines the words of sense(-making), visual and formers, referring to transformer and performer.

DOWNLOADABLE CONTENT

To help you Transform while Performing we created an inspiring resource and toolbox section on our Visual Senseformers website. This toolbox features a collection of free downloadable templates, which we have covered in this book, and we have brought together the best of the visuals into a single location.

Moreover, we've carefully curated these templates to ensure that they are visually appealing and easy to use.

Discover what we can do for you at **visualsenseformers.com.**

ABOUT THE AUTHORS

The Visual Senseformers

Kristof Braekeleire and Olivier Van Duüren each respectively worked twenty plus years for the headquarters of global technology giants and industry pioneers Hewlett-Packard and Microsoft. They know first-hand the pains of working in organisations that are constantly transforming. As independent entrepreneurs they currently advise start-ups and organisations in all major industries around the world.

They came to realise the old methods of building plans to Transform while Performing are simply not sufficient. To maximise their impact they founded the Visual Senseformers to help companies find their future North Star, build their strategic plan and get everyone to act in days, not months. They do this through coaching, keynotes, workshops and events unleashing the Power of 3: inspiration, visualisation and co-creation.

Author: Olivier Van Duüren

Olivier Van Duüren is an international public speaker, trend sensemaker, executive whisperer, transformer, active investor and author. After twenty-two years at Microsoft internationally, Olivier left to start The Dualarity, a book and a business, helping organisations to Transform while Performing. He teaches at the Zigurat Business School (University of Barcelona) for Technology and Innovation. He is an active investor of 9.5 Ventures building tailor-made start-ups for corporates, board member/advisor at various companies and co-founder of the Visual Senseformers.

Author & illustrator: Kristof Braekeleire

Kristof Braekeleire started drawing as a child and never stopped. Somewhere along the way he got into the tech business and spent twenty years at Hewlett-Packard, ending up working for the global headquarters in Silicon Valley as a visual strategist. In 2017 he left HP to start up JIXSO, a visual facilitation business, known for accelerating change and helping clients reach success quicker. His lifelong experience of drawing with his background in business and technology, allows him to merge his passion for problem-solving with his creative talent. He is co-founder of the Visual Senseformers.

Designer: Thomas Van Ryckeghem

Thomas Van Ryckeghem is a lecturer in Brand Identity, Graphic Design and Marketing at the University College Leuven Limburg. His passion lies in transforming a vision into a brand identity that truly resonates with people. Thomas eats logos for breakfast, branding for lunch, editorial design for afternoon tea and photography for dinner. He is also the author of the book Brand Design & Graphic Identity.

THANK YOU

First and foremost, we would like to thank you, our readers, for buying and reading this book. We wrote it for you.

You were our North Star during our writing journey. You helped us to stay the course.

Writing a book can be a daunting task, but co-authoring it, makes the whole journey not only less intimidating but also incredibly enriching and motivating. Share ideas and bounce off each other's perspectives turned the writing process very dynamic. And we had two sets of shoulders to carry the entire workload within a strict time frame. The result, we hope, is a well-rounded book.

We want to express our gratitude to everyone who contributed to this book staring with our pre-readers, who throughout the creation of this book, have helped us refine and polish our work, namely Stephen Quest, Andre Herman, Wouter Quartier, Erik Kerkhofs, Stijn Nauwelaerts, Thomas Van Duüren, Herman Spliethoff, Charles Hannaford, Peter Vindevogel, Madeline Martyn, Yves Van Rompaey, Maitri O'Brien and Martine Vanremoortele.

We would also like to extend our appreciation to all our customers who have shared their knowledge and expertise with us and have helped us refine our ideas during the many co-creation sessions. Several business leaders helped us shape and approve the publication of their business cases with full respect for the confidentiality of the used visuals.

We are deeply grateful to Debs Jenkins, our 'book smith', for being a partner in crime, for her wisdom, her invaluable guidance and for her enthusiastic belief in this project. Thank you Debs.

We would like to thank the whole team of BIS publishers for helping us to get the book on the market. Thank you Harm and team for placing your trust in us.

And because we wanted this book to be a visual and inspiring book, we knew we needed special attention for the lay out and graphic design, which is where Thomas Van Ryckeghem came in. Thank you, Thomas, for your hard work, patience and advice.

This book is a testament to the power of collaboration and we are honoured to have had the opportunity to work with such an amazing group of people. We want to thank everyone who motivated us to continue writing and sharing our learning and passion with the world.

Finally, we would like to thank our families for their unwavering love, patience and support.

Their encouragement and sacrifice has been invaluable to us during the entire process.

We hope that you, our readers, will find our collaboration as rewarding as we did.

REFERENCES

1. World Intellectual Property Organisation (WIPO), 2022, https://www.wipo.int/pressroom/en/articles/2022/article_0013.html#:~:text=Innovators%20around%20the%20world%20filed,67.6%25%20of%20all%20applications%20worldwide.

2. There is not much on the internet around this, but research has been done around this topic by Leontiev, Kaptelinin and Nardi. And when you google those, you run into topics like human activity, technology and interaction design, and interaction design is closely related the earliest forms of visual facilitation.

3. Leslie A. Perlow, Constance Noonan Hadley, Eunice Eun, Harvard Business Review, July-August 2017 issue (pp.62–69), Stop the Meeting Madness: How to free up time for meaningful work, https://hbr.org/2017/07/stop-the-meeting-madness.

4. Simon Sinek, Portfolio Penguin, 2009, Start with Why.

5. George T. Doran, Management Review, issue 1981, "There's a S.M.A.R.T. way to write management's goals and objectives." S.M.A.R.T. is an acronym listing criteria to help writing goals. It stands for Specific, Measurable, Achievable, Relevant, and Time-Bound. This approach eliminates generalities and guesswork, sets a clear timeline, and makes it easier to track progress and identify missed milestones.

6. Wikipedia, "A pole star or polar star is a star, preferably bright, nearly aligned with the axis of a rotating astronomical body. Currently, Earth's pole stars are Polaris (Alpha Ursae Minoris), also called the North Star, aligned approximately with its northern axis, and – on its southern axis – Polaris Australis (Sigma Octantis), a much dimmer star.".

7. Gapingvoid, September 13 2022, You Can't Go Far Without A North Star, https://www.gapingvoid.com/blog/2022/09/13/why-you-cant-go-far-without-a-north-star/.

8. Peter Hamilton Reynolds, Candlewick Press, 2009, The North Star. Reynolds is best known for his children's books about "authentic learning, creativity and self-expression", including The North Star, Ish, The Dot, and So Few of Me.

9. Bruce Jones, Harvard Business Review, February 2 2016, https://hbr.org/sponsored/2016/02/the-difference-between-purpose-and-mission.

10. Adam Bryant, The purpose of purpose, December 1, 2021, https://www.strategy-business.com/blog/The-purpose-of-purpose.

11. Simon Sinek, Portfolio, 2009, Start with Why: How Great Leaders Inspire Everyone to Take Action, is definitely a must read when trying to find your purpose. Sinek says people are inspired by a sense of purpose (or "Why"), and that this should come first when communicating, before "How" and "What".

12. E&Y, Corporate Board Global Leadership Forecast, 2019.

13. Xpheno, October 13, 2021, https://www.xpheno.com/blogs/the-biases-of-the-hybrid-workplace.

14. Hemant Kakkar, Subra Tangirala, Harvard Business Review, November 6, 2018, https://hbr.org/2018/11/if-your-employees-arent-speaking-up-blame-company-culture.

15. Peter Drucker, "Culture eats strategy for breakfast" is a famous quote attributed to the legendary Austrian-American management consultant and writer Peter Drucker. According to The Quote Investigator, this phrase first appeared on PIMA's North American Papermaker: The Official Publication of the Paper Industry Management Association, in an article by Bill Moore and Jerry Rose in 2000. Since then, the phrase has appeared many times. Peter Drucker died in 2005. The first time his name was associated to the citation was in 2011. Whoever said it is not important. The essence is not that strategy is unimportant, but rather that culture is what keeps employees motivated and clients happy, which greatly impacts company's success.

16. Online collaboration tools like https://www.mentimeter.com/ and https://www.slido.com/ are highly rated collaboration tools that allow users to engage and interact with the audience. Both cater to individual speakers, small and midsize businesses, and large enterprises.

17. Andrew D Brown, Ian Colville; Annie Pye, February 2015, , "Making Sense of Sensemaking in Organisation Studies", "There is no single agreed upon definition of sensemaking, but there is consensus that it is a process that allows people to understand ambiguous, equivocal or confusing issues or events." Organisation Studies 36 (2): 265–277. doi:10.1177/0170840614559259. ISSN 0170-8406.

18. ChatGPT (short for "Conversational Generative Pre-training Transformer") is a machine learning model developed by OpenAI that generates human-like text.

19. The phrase "a vision without action is a dream, a dream without vision is a nightmare" is a variation of a Japanese proverb that goes "Vision without action is a daydream; action without vision is a nightmare."

20. Victoria C. Oleynick, Todd M. Thrash, Michael C. LeFew, Emil G. Moldovan, Paul D. Kieffaber, Frontiers in Human Neuroscience, June 25, 2014, The scientific study of inspiration in the creative process: challenges and opportunities, https://www.ncbi.nlm.nih.gov/pmc/articles/PMC4070479/.

21. David Sibbet, 2001, Sibbet wrote an article "A Graphic Facilitation Retrospective", telling the story of early pioneers of graphic facilitation who were inspired by architects (with understanding of large imagery), designers, computer engineers (who started to cluster information in a new way). Sibbet described that what at a glance "just" looked like graphics was much more: "It was also dance, and story telling, since the facilitator was constantly in physical motion, miming the group and its

communication with movement, as well as commenting on the displays, suggesting processes and the like." An early paper in the field of graphic facilitation was "Explicit Group Memory" by Geoff Ball, who claimed that a shared picture is the best way to support group learning or, more importantly, a lasting memory in the group.

22. The International Forum of Visual Practitioners (IFVP) is an international forum with hundreds of members all over the planet. As an organisation, they offer educational programmes and conferences for members work to advance the field of visual practice. https://ifvp.org.

23. Venkat Ramaswamy, Francis Gouillart, Harvard Business Review, October 2010, https://hbr.org/2010/10/building-the-co-creative-enterprise.

24. Xplane, November 28, 2016, https://xplane.com/a-brief-history-of-co-creation/.

25. Fishbowl is a powerful technique for organising medium- to large-group discussions. Participants are separated into an inner and outer circle. In the inner circle or fishbowl, participants, the fish, have a discussion. The ones in the outer circle listen to the discussion but can't speak or interrupt. Anyone can join the inner circle and take part in the discussion if they replace one of the members in the inner circle. This happens by tapping one of the fish on the shoulder after which they take his or her place. The advantage of fishbowl is that it creates a safe environment allowing the entire group to join the discussion if they feel like it.

26. The HP/HPE Envision practice was a global transformation practice that helped HP's top clients visualise their strategic business outcomes and develop prioritised action plans, co-created with senior stakeholders of both the client and HP/HPE.

27. Helen Phillips, Newscientist, September 4, 2006, https://www.newscientist.com/article/dn9969-introduction-the-human-brain/.

28. Carol S. Dweck Ph.D, Random House Publishing Group, February 28. 2006, Mindset: The New Psychology of Success

29. Satya Nadella, CEO Microsoft, The Wall Street Journal, January 1, 2019, https://www.wsj.com/video/satya-nadella-the-learn-it-all-does-better-than-the-know-it-all/D8BC205C-D7F5-423E-8A41-0E921E86597C.html.

30. Carol S. Dweck Ph.D, Random House Publishing Group, February 28. 2006, Mindset: The New Psychology of Success, "In a growth mindset, people believe that their most basic abilities can be developed through dedication and hard work – brains and talent are just the starting point. This view creates a love of learning and a resilience that is essential for great accomplishment.".

31. Patrick Lencioni, Jossey-Bass, April 11, 2002, The Five Dysfunctions of a Team.

32. Carmine Gallo, St. Martin's Press, March 4, 2014, How to talk like TED.

33. Sting. A line from the song "An Englishman in New York".

34. Steve Jobs, Apple, November 2003, quoted when talking about the iPod's second anniversary of its release.

35. Marc A. Feigen, Michael Jenkins, Anton Warendh, Harvard Business Review, July-August 2022, https://hbr.org/2022/07/is-it-time-to-consider-co-ceos.

36. Strategyzer, Alexander Osterwalder, Yves Pigneur, Wiley, 2020, The Invincible Company.

37. Strategyzer, Alexander Osterwalder, March 30, 2017, https://www.strategyzer.com/blog/why-every-company-needs-a-chief-entrepreneur.

38. Lisa Kay Solomon, January 11, 2018, https://www.lisakaysolomon.com/resources/2018/4/13/how-the-most-successful-leaders-will-thrive-in-an-exponential-world-1.

39. Statler and Waldorf are a pair of grumpy old muppets best known for their loud, opinionated and unfriendly statements. The two elderly men first appeared in The Muppet Show in 1975, where they consistently make rude and mocking remarks about the performance from their balcony seats.

40. Translated from an article in De Tijd, October 18, 2022, https://www.tijd.be/dossiers/de-tijdcapsule/neuhaus-ceo-ignace-van-doorselaere-bestuursleden-zijn-soms-als-statler-en-waldorf/10421168.

41. Paul Leinwand, Mahadeva Matt Mani, Blair Sheppard, Harvard Business Review, January-February 2022, https://hbr.org/2022/01/reinventing-your-leadership-team.

42. Tendayi Viki, April 15 2016, https://tendayiviki.com/why-rd-spending-is-not-a-measure-of-innovation/.

43. Alex Osterwalder, Strategyzer, Business Model Generation.

44. Gary P. Pisano, Harvard Business Review, January-February 2019, https://hbr.org/2019/01/the-hard-truth-about-innovative-cultures.

45. Harvard Business Review, July-August 2019, https://hbr.org/2019/07/the-wrong-ways-to-strengthen-culture - https://www.forbes.com/sites/davidrock/2019/05/24/fastest-way-to-change-culture/?sh=58399cac3d50.

46. Gartner, Newsroom, September 20, 2018, https://www.gartner.com/en/newsroom/press-releases/2018-09-20-gartner-says-only-31-percent-of-hr-leaders-believe-their-organisations-have-the-culture-necessary-to-drive-performance.

47. Neuroleadership Institute, https://neuroleadershipinstitute.org/solutions-for-organisations/culture-leadership/.

48. Bryan Walker, Sarah A. Soule, Harvard Business Review, June 20, 2017, https://hbr.org/2017/06/changing-company-culture-requires-a-movement-not-a-mandate.

49. Growth Mindset Institute, https://www.growthmindsetinstitute.org/.

50. Growth Mindset Institute, https://www.growthmindsetinstitute.org/growth-mindset/growth-mindset-for-business/mindset-assessment/

51. Umicore, https://www.umicore.com/en/.

52. Scott D. Anthony, Paul Cobban, Rahul Nair, Natalie Painchaud, Harvard Business Review, November-December 2019, https://hbr.org/2019/11/breaking-down-the-barriers-to-innovation.